AGRARIAN CLASS CONFLICT

University of British Columbia Press
Asian Studies Monographs

Agrarian Class Conflict is the second volume in a continuing series of studies in Asian history and society published by the University of British Columbia Press.

Other volumes in the series are:
1. *China's Intellectual Dilemma: Politics and University Enrolment, 1949-1978,* by Robert Taylor

AGRARIAN CLASS CONFLICT

THE POLITICAL MOBILIZATION OF AGRICULTURAL LABOURERS IN KUTTANAD, SOUTH INDIA

Joseph Tharamangalam

UNIVERSITY OF BRITISH COLUMBIA PRESS
VANCOUVER AND LONDON

AGRARIAN CLASS CONFLICT

*The Political Mobilization of Agricultural Labourers
in Kuttanad, South India*

This book has been published with the assistance of a grant from the Social Science Federation of Canada, using funds provided by the Social Sciences and Humanities Research Council of Canada.

Tharamangalam, Joseph.
  Agrarian class conflict

  (Asian studies monographs; 2)
  Bibliography: p.
  Includes index.
  ISBN 0-7748-0126-3

1. Agricultural laborers—India—Kuttanad—Political activity.
2. Trade-unions—Agricultural laborers—India—Kuttanad. 3. Social
classes—India—Kuttanad. I. Title. II. Series.
HD1537.14T492   331.7'63'095483   C80-091229-2

International Standard Book Number 0-7748-0126-3

Printed in Canada

Contents

Tables

Preface and Acknowledgements

This book is a revised version of a doctoral thesis submitted to the department of sociology at York University. Fieldwork for this study was conducted in 1974-75, and most of the chapters were written in 1975-76. It, therefore, describes events and processes that took place before August 1975. Although I conducted further fieldwork in 1979-80, I have resisted the temptation to update the book for two main reasons. First, significant economic and political changes have occurred in Kuttanad since 1975, which include a substantial fall in paddy prices during the last few years and a recent rapprochement between the CPI and the CPI(M). These would require detailed treatment and hence a much larger book, if not an altogether new one. Not only do I lack the time and resources for this task at this time, but this book, already in press for two years, can wait no longer. Second, despite these changes, I see little reason at this time to make any substantial alteration in my basic arguments or conclusions.

This book is dedicated to the landless agricultural labourers of Kuttanad. For centuries, they were passive objects of history, acted upon by external forces, by other men and other classes. Now, through their courageous struggle for elementary human dignity they have transformed themselves into active agents for historical change with some collective power, however limited, to change their condition, and in the process Indian society itself.

Many people have helped in the preparation and publication of this book. I am grateful to the Shastri Indo-Canadian Institute for granting me a junior fellowship which made the fieldwork in India possible. I wish to thank my former teachers, Professors Anton H. Turrittin, Donald Willmott, and Mirek Disman for their help and guidance in the planning and writing of this work when it was a thesis. I also warmly thank Kathleen Gough, who gave me her valuable time and advice at various stages of this work. Finally, it is difficult to talk about this work without thanking Elzy Tharamangalam for her loving support, without which it would never have been completed.

1

Introduction

The vast majority of mankind lives in agrarian societies in the so-called underdeveloped countries of the third world. Yet it was not until recently that sociologists and anthropologists began to give any systematic attention to these societies. To be sure, anthropologists and ethnologists have long been carrying out studies of tribes, primitives, and even peasants, no doubt taking special care to record their exotic customs and strange cultural traits. But it has been the peasant wars and upheavals of the twentieth century that have captured the attention of social scientists and turned their thoughts seriously to the political and revolutionary potential of the peasantries of the world and to the implications of this potential for the future of mankind.[1] Sociologists and anthropologists, who entered the field relatively late,[2] have been able to generate much greater interest in the nature of these societies, in their internal differentiation and dynamics, and in the impact on these societies of exogenous, worldwide processes.[3] Greater attention has also been given to discovering general patterns and regularities regarding these phenomena. A major concern for the political sociology of the rural communities of the non-Western world has been to discover the general conditions under which peasants rise in revolt or become politically mobilized and the conditions under which they are able to achieve at least limited success.

One aspect of agrarian societies that has received greater recognition as a result of these concerns is the degree to which they are internally differentiated. Gone is the idyllic notion of the harmonious ''peasant community.''[4] Gone also is the image of the isolated and self-sufficient ''village community.''[5] It has now become clear that there are few peasant communities even in the remotest corners of the world which have been left untouched by the upheavals and turmoils that created the modern industrial world. The metropolitan centres of the world have throughout maintained an organic relationship to the hinterlands in Asia, Africa,

Latin America, and Oceania.[6] Everywhere the spread of world capitalism has disrupted the traditional institutions and cultures of ancient societies and destroyed the age-old certainties and customary securities of their peasant populations. Capitalism undermined the power and privileges of ancient elites and created inequalities and human exploitation the extent and scale of which were hitherto unknown. Social scientists have, belatedly, focused some attention on the political orientations of different agrarian classes, their responses to these dislocations, and their respective roles in revolutions.[7] In a well-known study of the peasant wars of the twentieth century, Eric Wolf has documented how each of these revolutions was a direct response to the massive disruptions caused by the intrusion of world capitalism. However, few studies have focused specifically on the last group in the chain of capitalist exploitation—the landless labourers, or the rural proletariat, in the underdeveloped countries.[8] Yet, there is increasing evidence that, as the processes of capitalist development continue to penetrate the remotest corners of the globe, this underclass is not only increasing in numbers, but also increasingly becoming restless and mobilized for political action.[9] It seems likely that this class will play a greater and more important role in agrarian movements in the years to come.

Recent evidence from India suggests that it is no exception to this general trend. Since the mid-1960's, not only have agrarian conflicts been on the increase in various parts of the country, but the new conflicts are of a different kind; they now involve neither factions cutting across classes nor even landlords and tenants as in the past, but landless labourers and their employers. The significance of this phenomenon becomes evident when it is realized that in 1971 agricultural labourers accounted for 25.7 per cent of all workers and 37 per cent of all agriculturalists. Kerala, like the rest of south India, has a much higher proportion of agricultural labourers, the figures being 30.68 per cent and 62 per cent respectively.[10] As we shall see shortly, there are regions, among which is Kuttanad, where the percentage has reached crisis proportions.

This study is concerned with agrarian class conflict in India. More specifically, it is meant to be a contribution to our understanding of the rural proletariat and its struggles. It hopes to achieve this goal by examining in detail the agricultural labour movement in Kuttanad, a paddy-growing backwater area lying on the southwest coast of India, in the state of Kerala. The choice of Kuttanad has not been a random one. One of the two "rice bowls" of Kerala, Kuttanad became notorious for the high levels of its agrarian unrest during the 1960's. The seriousness of the situation can be judged from the fact that between 1965 and 1971 few agricultural operations in this region, especially harvesting, took place without the massive presence of the police. This situation has resulted from the struggles between Kuttanad's large agricultural labour force, representing two-thirds of its agricultural population, and the employers of their labour, who make up the remaining one-third of this population. During the past four decades the agricultural labourers of Kuttanad have emerged to occupy the centre of the political scene in the region and have become a politically explosive force. To my knowledge, they were the first in the country to organize an agricultural labour union, and today Kuttanad can claim to have the best organized and politicized of such unions in the country. Kuttanad has other characteristics that make it an ideal place in which to observe the agrarian upheavals that are enveloping many parts of the Indian countryside. These will be fully described in the next chapter. Here it will suffice to state simply that it is a microcosm in which elements that make up India's agrarian problem can be closely observed at a relatively advanced stage—high population density, capitalist farming, a sharply polarized agricultural population with a high proportion of landless labourers, and a relatively literate and awakened population.

The assumptions implicit in the special place claimed for Kuttanad are obvious. There is, first, the assumption that certain structural characteristics are associated with agrarian class conflict, and, second, there is the further assumption that the study of Kuttanad can say something in general about such conflicts because these structural characteristics are present there in a particularly strong form. Kuttanad, then, is not simply a *typical* case, but perhaps if the use of the term is permitted, an *archetypal* case. This statement requires some further comment. In the first place, a number of recent studies which have analyzed the structural roots of agrarian conflict point out that significant changes are occurring in the agrarian structure of India as a result of many factors, the most important of these being land reform, commercial farming, and the so-called Green Revolution. Quite apart from population increase, these studies suggest an increase in rural inequality and a greater polarization of the agrarian class structure.[11] All these changes appeared in Kuttanad earlier and in a relatively acute form. Kuttanad is also an Intensive Agricultural District Programme (IADP) area, where the Green Revolution "package" has been tried with some success. Secondly, the areas in India where agrarian conflicts have appeared in the most intense and advanced form during the past two decades share some specific features—in general, they are in the densely populated coastal areas of wet paddy cultivation.[12] Even among these areas, Kuttanad stands out as embodying all these features in their sharpest form. There seem to be strong grounds, therefore, for assuming that the study of agrarian class conflict in Kuttanad can throw a good deal of light on agrarian class conflict in India in general. It must be stressed, however, that Kuttanad is only a small region in a small state in India. In order to arrive at useful and significant generalizations we need many empirical studies of other areas with which Kuttanad can be compared and contrasted.

The mobilization of the agricultural labourers of Kuttanad has been both difficult and of great significance. Four decades ago they were the poorest, the most illiterate, the least organized, and the most exploited group of people in the region, belonging largely to the untouchable and backward castes, with centuries of tradition of social degradation and deference to their masters. Moreover, they were divided among themselves by caste (the untouchables themselves belonged to several sub-castes) and "patron-client" bondage. Loyalties ran vertically between them and their employer-masters through the system of patronage and not horizontally within their class or even caste. It is not surprising that revolutionary leaders and theoreticians have generally tended not to give any serious attention to the revolutionary or political potential of this class. Yet, today none except those blinded by ideology can ignore the organized strength of the agricultural labourers in Kuttanad, although its extent and long term political and revolutionary significance may be in question. And despite the views of those who attribute such developments to the machinations of "outside agitators" and "unscrupulous politicians," it must be assumed that, given certain favourable conditions, even landless labourers will use the resources at their command to organize and to protect their interests. Such an assumption has always been implicit in Marxian sociology. One of the major aims of this study is to discern what precisely those conditions or conjuncture of conditions were and how these have influenced events in Kuttanad society.

DEFINING THE PROBLEM

This study examines the mobilization and the organized struggles of the agricultural labourers of Kuttanad to achieve higher wages, better working conditions, and, above all, human dignity. This movement entailed the growth of the self-awareness of the agricultural labourers, took shape at a particular historical period and under concrete historical conditions, and involved struggles against another distinct group of people in Kuttanad, their employers and "masters," a group which both exploited and dominated them. It is evident that the agricultural labour movement involved significant processes of social conflict and historical change with important implications for the transformation of social relations and social consciousness in Kuttanad society. As has been observed, this was indeed a pioneering movement for agricultural labourers at the time, but since then, and particularly in recent years, such movements have appeared elsewhere both in and outside Kerala. An important problem for the sociologist is how to identify the conditions or factors that can account for these developments.

Admittedly, these are complex processes, and there are many factors that must be taken into account for an adequate understanding of them, not the least of which is the presence of a communist party or movement committed to organizing workers and peasants for what it conceives to be the inevitable class struggle.[13] But the questions still remain. Why did the party go to Kuttanad and not elsewhere? Why did it go to Kuttanad at the particular time that it did? Why did it organize agricultural labourers and not other sections of the agricultural population? Perhaps, the party tried all or most of these, but its message struck such a responsive chord only among the agricultural labourers of Kuttanad at the particular time it did. If this is the case, why was this so? Again, what concrete course of development did the movement follow and why? And finally, what are the implications of the movement for the transformation of Kuttanad's class structure and of its social structure itself?

The answers provided by this study to these questions will depend upon the formulation of the central problem, which will focus on the nature and dynamics of agrarian class struggle in Kuttanad. At the highest level of abstraction, the problem concerns the relationship between social structure and politics. Since politics is concerned with the articulation and promotion of conflicting group interests, the problem can be formulated in terms of uncovering the social basis of conflicts and the social organization of conflicting interests. More specifically, two aspects of the question can be distinguished. The first concerns the structural roots of conflict, that is, the objective formation and changes in the class structure of Kuttanad society which are predicated on the development of its productive forces. The second concerns the social dynamics of conflict, that is, the more subjective processes of the mobilization, organization, and struggles of the exploited class which are premised on the development of class consciousness. Both these processes are dependent on many factors, some intrinsic and some extrinsic. Thus, ecological, technological, and demographic factors have greatly influenced the concrete class structure of Kuttanad. It is also clear that Kuttanad society has been profoundly influenced by wider social, economic, and political processes, in particular by the penetration of capitalism and its market relations. Hence, it is necessary to place particular emphasis on the dialectical process by which historically determined structural and cultural factors interact to form the specific kind of class relations, consciousness, and conflict that inform Kuttanad society today. Class struggle is an historical phenomenon, and the two aspects of it are dialectically related. The objective factors of commonality of situation and of interest become subjectively perceived by the actors at a particular historical period and under certain conditions. In the process of transition from the first phase to the second there are many factors involved; the process is likely to be mediated through such primordial loyalties and institutions as caste and kinship.[14]

Concretely, this inquiry will focus on two processes: first, the class structure of Kuttanad, stressing especially the emergence of a rural proletariat with great potential for radical political action, and second, the political mobilization of the agricultural labour class, the rural proletariat—its struggles and its transformation from a category of people, divided by caste and patron-client bondage, to a class, organized, politically conscious, and engaged in struggle. In terms of Marxian theoretical categories our point of departure will be the problematic comprehended in the transformation of a class ''in itself'' to a class ''for itself'' and the historical and structural conditions involved in this process.

THEORETICAL APPROACHES: THE TRADITIONAL MODELS

Kuhn has shown that the formulation of scientific problems, to say nothing of their treatment, is constrained and limited by the "paradigms" prevalent within a given scientific community.[15] It is not surprising that social scientists operating with essentially functionalist paradigms have failed to formulate adequately the problem of conflict and its dynamics in agrarian societies in general and in rural India in particular. Some of the important paradigms used in dealing with rural India have been those of the "village community," the "peasant community," the "caste society," and in the case of political scientists, "pluralist democracy" that functions through "interest group politics." Among these paradigms there are two which deserve particular attention, those of the peasant community and the caste society.

Interest in the so-called peasant communities was sparked by the works of Robert Redfield and his colleagues. The application of the anthropological method of fieldwork to peasant communities may have salvaged anthropology from running out of its traditional subject, the tribes, giving the discipline at the same time wider relevance and greater respectability.[16] What is important to note here is that while these anthropologists analyzed the links between the peasant community and the outside world, they also presented a largely utopian and idyllic picture of it, overemphasizing its homogeneity, shared values, openness, mutual interdependence, and harmony. Such a conception of society was later shown to be inadequate even for the village studied by Redfield.[17] However, this tradition acquired widespread popularity, influencing the study of village and peasant communities in many countries, including India and China.[18]

It must be noted that the problem of class and class conflict in peasant societies continued to be neglected despite the fact that concern with these societies had brought the disciplines of sociology and anthropology together. A child of the industrial and political revolutions in Europe, sociology had laid much stress on class, conflict, and change. Yet, it soon overwhelmingly accepted and continues to accept the functionalist framework as appropriate and perhaps comfortable for analyzing both industrial and non-industrial societies. The failure to take into account the cleavages and conflicts in peasant societies is all the more surprising when looked at with the wisdom of hindsight—with the knowledge of the peasant wars that have occurred since in some of the same societies studied by these scholars. Even today, however, there does not appear to be any radical rethinking of the conceptual framework for the study of these societies in mainstream sociology and anthropology.

The greatest influence in the study of Indian rural society has been exerted by the model of the caste society. The preoccupation with caste may have many causes. Perhaps the uniqueness and the exotic character of the institution caught the attention of non-Indian social scientists.[20] Perhaps the conceptual approaches to the study of inequality inherited by most sociologists were in harmony with the prevalent conceptions of caste. At any rate, it is now conceded by many students of Indian society that the preoccupation with caste has led to serious distortions in our understanding of rural Indian society by overemphasizing some of its features and by underestimating, if not completely ignoring, others.[21] Thus, in the first place, the model tends to give a certain primary importance to ideology, religious values, and norms and underemphasizes the strivings and doings of people and the material conditions of their daily lives.[22] Second, it assumes the existence of consensus on these stated norms and values, and therefore it takes little account of both the conflicts underlying the structure and the phenomenon of power and coercion that may be at least equally important in upholding it. Third, it views the different castes that constitute the basic units in the system as being mutually complementary and non-antagonistic. Fourth, it takes the Indian system of inequality to be a rigid and relatively static system of social ranking.[23]

It should be pointed out that the two models of Indian society discussed above have much in common. The peasant model stresses homogeneity, harmony, and the *gemeinschaft* aspects of rural society; the caste model explicitly recognizes important cleavages in society, but treats these in terms of complementarity, functional interdependence, and shared values. Both represent the conservative thesis regarding social stratification as explained by Lenski,[24] and both employ what Ossowski has termed the functional scheme in describing different groups in society.[25] Both tend to define social structure by cultural norms and jural rules. It is clear that both the models bypass the problem of class analysis and fail to examine the material basis of inequality. The crucial questions of landownership and the exercise of power are treated, if at all, indirectly in terms of landowning castes and landless castes, or dominant castes and subject castes. Yet, as Myrdal has noted, ''particularly in the south Asian rural setting, inequality is, in fact, mainly a question of landownership—with which are associated leisure, enjoyment of status and authority. Income differences are considered less significant.''[26] Both models seem clearly inadequate in explaining conflict and change. It is true that conflicts have not been completely ignored by scholars working in these traditions. But when these are dealt with, they have generally been treated under the rubric of factionalism or of ''interest group politics.''[27] It must be conceded that factionalism and even vertical mobilization of the rural population behind upper-caste village elites are of considerable importance in rural India even today. But factionalism is not an adequate concept to deal with the major conflicts that are now enveloping the Indian countryside. The emerging struggles between the landless and the landowners, between agricultural labourers and their employers, and in many places between the tenants and the landlords are struggles between classes and are of much greater significance in terms of the immense effects they have on the nature of Indian society. Nor can these be adequately comprehended within the model of ''pluralist democracy'' adopted by political scientists and political sociologists. In this model, interest group politics is seen as accommodating conflict and promoting democracy.[28]

However, it fails to deal adequately with the structural roots and dynamics of rural conflict. Evidently, a more adequate conceptual framework for the explanation and understanding of these phenomena is needed. In the following section, the suitability at the Marxian model to serve as such a framework will be considered.

CLASS AND CLASS CONFLICT: THE MARXIAN MODEL

The central concerns of Marxian sociological analysis have been the structural differentiation of societies into antagonistic classes and the dynamics of social change and transformation inherent in conflicting class interests, the concept of structure being defined in terms of the mode and relations of production. Giddens has recently claimed that academic sociology, in its classical European form, has always considered the problem of class and class conflict as the central problem, indeed the only problem, in sociological analysis.[29]

It is well known that Marx never gave a formal definition of the concept of class and that his final and systematic presentation of the topic remained unfinished. Nevertheless, the broad outlines of his conception are not difficult to trace.[30]

1) Class is an analytic concept and must be distinguished from such descriptive terms as income group, stratum, caste, or estate. The analytic value of the concept derives from the fact that it forms part of a theory of social structure, social conflict, and historical change. Stratification systems, that is, the ranking of social groups in a scale of higher and lower social positions, are secondary and derived from the fundamental fact of the class character of a society.

2) Classes are historical categories and exist in concrete, historically constituted social formations. Classes constitute and define the concrete structure of a given society and also act as the driving force for its transformation. Class is, therefore, a dynamic and not a static concept.

3) Classes are relational. A class exists only in relation to another class or to other classes, thus forming a class *system*. The relationship between the classes is asymmetrical, antagonistic, and dialectical. It is this relationship that defines the nature of the classes and helps mold social structure itself. A class society is inherently unstable because of the contingent nature of the relationship between the classes and the tension between them.

4) Since social classes are not defined by secondary criteria, such as income or status, they are not coterminous with strata arising from the division of labour. They are defined by the fundamental criterion of relationship to the means of production. It was Lenin rather than Marx who attempted to spell out the Marxist conception of class. According to him,

classes are large groups of people which differ from each other by the place they occupy in a historically determined system of social production, by their relation (in most cases fixed and formulated in law) to the means of production, by their role in the social organization of labour, and consequently, by the dimension and mode of acquiring the share of social wealth of which they dispose. Classes are groups of people one of which can appropriate the labour of another owing to the different places they occupy in a definite system of social economy.[31]

The class model is predicated on the theory of surplus value which, at bottom, states the universal truth that in all known societies a minority has been able to live at the expense of the labour of the rest of the population. Control over the means of production is strategic because it enables the minority to compel others to work and to extract the surplus produced by them.

5) The antagonistic relations between classes manifest themselves at all levels of society, above all in the economic and political spheres. Consequently, they form definite politico-economic interest groups with the potential of transforming themselves into political groups engaged in struggle.

6) The most important phase in the development of class is that of class struggle which, in turn, is predicated on the development of class consciousness. Strictly speaking, class, in the objective sense in which we have described it above, does not yet constitute a sociological group in that it has no sense of its own identity and no consciousness of its class interests. It is only a class "in itself" and is incapable of any organized or collective action to change its "class situation," and consequently the social structure. It becomes politically significant when it attains a consciousness of itself as a class and an awareness of its interests, that is, when it becomes a class "for itself." Class consciousness manifests itself when a class is politically mobilized and organized for struggle.

The problematic comprehended in the distinction between a class "in itself" and a class "for itself" is central to a Marxian political sociology. At the most abstract level, the question concerns the relationship between class and politics. Obviously the question has no significance for those who look to national character or cultural traditions to understand political behaviour. An implicit assumption in Marxian thinking is that given the appropriate conjuncture of favourable historical and structural conditions a class is likely to organize in order to defend its interests. It is in this historical process that a class "in itself" becomes transformed into a class "for itself." The task of the sociologist, then, is to analyze the dynamics of the transformation of the one to the other and to identify the concrete conjuncture of conditions in which such a transformation takes place.

It must be pointed out that the concept of class consciousness is one of the most complex and ambiguous ones in Marxian sociology. The notion that a class has an objective common interest of which its members are not aware is one that many find difficult to accept.[32] Yet, history is replete with examples of "sleeping giants," of long oppressed but seemingly inactive and uncomplaining groups suddenly rising in revolt.[33] Moreover, given the analytical nature of the concept, there is no reason why the sociologist cannot use it fruitfully. It can enable him to analyze the processes involved in the mobilization of classes for collective action. It must be noted that for Marx the two phases in the development of classes are consecutive because men's social consciousness is determined by their social conditions. Nevertheless, the transition from one to the other is not automatic, nor does every group organized for political action have class as its basis. There is a dilemma in the Marxian theory of class consciousness. On the one hand, both class consciousness and the possibility of the revolution are premised on the internal contradictions of capitalism, which are independent of the consciousness and will of the actors in the system. On the other hand, there is the recognized need for a political organization of the working class in order to achieve these goals. In practice, few revolutionaries have relied on the spontaneity of the working class; theoreticians of the revolution such as Lenin and Gramsci have especially stressed the necessity to create effective working class organizations.[34] However, it has now been convincingly shown by Mészaros, among others, that the dilemma is more apparent than real: Marxism subscribes to neither mechanical determinism nor voluntarism. The relationship between class and politics, the so-called substructure and superstructure, is not a simple one of determinant and determined, but a complex and dialectical one. It must be remembered that the rationale behind Marx's revolt against Hegelian idealism was his effort to wrest the determining role in human history from any transcendental principle or abstract consciousness, and to place it in human praxis and therefore within human history itself. As Mészaros has pointed out, "economic relations do not exist outside the historically changing complex of mediations, including the most 'spiritual' ones."[35]

It is clear, however, that the empirical analysis of class consciousness is beset with problems. Class consciousness is not an either/or phenomenon. It exists at different levels and in varying degrees. It may range, for instance, between an awareness of a commonality of economic and social situation to a revolutionary consciousness that questions the legitimacy of the prevailing social structure and holds out alternative possibilities.[36] Hence, the sociologist cannot attempt an adequate examination of the phenomenon without, at the least, distinguishing the levels and degrees of class consciousness. There is the further problem of operationalizing the concept in order to identify and measure the degrees of its empirical manifestation. This requires identifiable and measurable indices. The aims of the present study are modest in this respect. The focus will be on the dynamics of the agricultural labour movement and on the mobilization and struggles of the agricultural labour class. The discussion of class consciousness will be in the context of these—class consciousness as implied, embodied, and manifested in the organized struggles of the agricultural labourers. The assumption is that the intensity of conflict and the level and extent of participation by the labourers are indices of their class consciousness.

RELEVANCE OF THE MARXIAN MODEL TO INDIA

The Marxian model was formulated for the analysis of Western capitalism, a social formation to which Marx, like all other classical sociologists, devoted most of his attention.[37] It is not surprising that he focused his attention especially on the two rising classes, the bourgeoisie and the proletariat, and considered the peasantry to be marginal. In an often-quoted passage Marx observed that the great mass of the French nation, the French peasantry, "is formed by simple addition of homologous magnitudes, much as potatoes in a sack form a sack of potatoes." Objectively, argued Marx, they formed a class, but in so far as "the identity of their interests begets no community, no national bond and no political organization among them, they do not form a class . . . [and] are consequently incapable of representing their own interests."[38] This passage is often used as a basis to contend that Marx held a negative view about the political potential of the peasantry in general. However, Marx's statement referred specifically to the small-holding French peasantry of Napoleonic France; nothing can be more erroneous than to treat it as a universal and absolute statement about the peasantry regardless of time and place. As Alavi has aptly remarked, "ascription of absolute characteristics to any group, regardless of historical contexts is alien to the Marxist method."[39] In any case, to later Marxists in Russia and eastern Europe, the peasantry was crucial, and the "differentiation" question as well as the revolutionary potential of the peasantry became central to the political debate. It is not surprising, therefore, that the classical Marxist theoretician on the peasantry and on the "agrarian question" is Lenin rather than Marx. The greatest merit of Lenin's approach was that he set aside the prevalent cultural definitions of the peasantry and utopian views of the Russian peasant commune and formulated a Marxian model for the analysis of peasant classes. To him the Narodnik view that the peasant commune was a potential and incipient form of socialist community was an implicit justification for the exploitation of one peasant class by another.

Lenin's subdivision of the Russian peasantry into three classes is well known:

1) *kulak,* or the rich peasant;
2) *stredniak,* or the middle peasant; and
3) *bedniak,* or the poor peasant.

Lenin's work on the peasantry was part of a major study of the development of capitalism in Russia.[40] Like Marx, Lenin was concerned with understanding the development of capitalism, in this case, in Russian agriculture. Hence, he laid great stress on the new classes, which he regarded as forces for the dissolution of the feudal order. He wrote

> The old peasantry is not only 'differentiating', it is being completely dissolved, it is ceasing to exist, it is being ousted by completely new types of inhabitants—types that are the basis of a society in which commodity economy and capitalist production prevail. These types are the rural bourgeoisie (chiefly petty bourgeoisie) and the rural proletariat—a class of commodity producers in agriculture and a class of agricultural wage labourers.[41]

Needless to say, the middle peasant not only does not belong to the same economic "sector," but is a "disintegrating" class.

Lenin's conceptual scheme provided a model for most subsequent analyses of rural classes among Marxist writers. Mao Tse-tung initially elaborated further on Lenin's categories but later reverted to the simpler classification.[42] Thus in 1933 he divided Chinese rural society into five classes, adding to Lenin's three peasant classes the landlord at the top and the rural wage labourer at the bottom.[43] In analyzing agrarian classes in India the Communist Party of India (Marxist), or CPI(M) uses the Maoist model with one modification: it divides the landlords into feudal and capitalist, apparently on the basis of the source of their income, thus arriving at a six-fold scheme. A landlord is classified as feudal if his income from rent is greater than his income from wage exploitation. And the distinction between a rich peasant and a landlord derives from the fact that the former (or members of his family) participates in agricultural operations through manual labour while the latter relies wholly on wage labour.[44] Later, some of the problems involved in a Marxian analysis of agrarian classes in Kuttanad will be discussed. For the moment it suffices to state that the Leninist categories have been used by many as statistical rather than sociological ones, that is, those differentiated on the basis of simple differences in wealth or amount of land owned. Lenin himself does not seem to have been altogether without fault in this regard. His category of poor peasants consisted not only of the rural proletariat but of the rural poor in general. Alavi is one of the few scholars who have attempted to differentiate peasant classes strictly on the basis of their position in the organization of production. In the "transitional historical situations," of which he assumes India to be a case, he distinguishes three "sectors" of the rural economy, and two modes of production. In the first sector, land is owned by landlords but cultivated by landless tenants, mostly sharecroppers who are classed as poor peasants. The second sector is that of the middle peasants, the independent small-holders who neither employ labour nor work as labourers themselves. In the third sector are the capitalist farmers who carry on cultivation by the exploitation of wage labour. Thus there are capitalist farmers, independent small-holders, sharecroppers, and farm labourers. Having made this classification, however, Alavi reverts back to the three classes, rich peasants, middle peasants and poor peasants, in order to conform to traditional usage.[45] Alavi's classes are scientific and precise, but as will become clear later, not applicable to Kuttanad or south India, nor probably to any part of India.

The question about the rural class structure cannot be resolved without first resolving a more fundamental debate on the mode of production in agriculture. Is India's agriculture capitalist, feudalist, or semi-feudalist? Alavi's analysis is premised on the existence of two modes of production. As a result of criticisms and continuing debate, Alavi later gave up his "sectoral" or "two modes of production" approach, arguing that the social and economic structure of India and other third-world countries could be best understood by employing the framework of a "colonial mode of production."[46] The majority of Indian Marxists, however, still employ some version of the dual-economy thesis. Nonetheless, the dual-economy thesis has not proven to be a satisfactory one. Why it is not suitable for understanding Kuttanad's class structure will be discussed in Chapter 3. While capitalism has penetrated all corners of the earth, it has penetrated Kuttanad more deeply and for a longer period of time than most other regions in the country (with the exception, of course, of cash crop plantations) and polarized the agrarian population quite sharply.

Another important problem for a Marxian analysis of class and class conflict in the so-called traditional societies arises because of the way in which economic relations there are "embedded" in social institutions forming part of kinship, political, religious, and other obligations.[47] This contrasts sharply with nineteenth-century capitalism, in which economic relations had achieved a certain degree of autonomy from these institutions. Marx himself held that it was this "emancipation" of the economic sphere that made both commodity production and wage labour possible. It is easy to see that where such emancipation has not taken place class relations are much less transparent and are submerged or embedded within primordial loyalties and institutions. The problem has been aptly posed by Godelier, a Marxian anthropologist, in relation to the analysis of kinship in Africa: "How, within Marx's perspective, can we understand both the *dominant* role of kinship and the determining role of the economy in the last instance?"[48] It is clear that the major problem in this regard for Indian society will be not kinship but caste and its relation to the class structure.

The first step in understanding the concrete relationship between class and caste is the demystification of the latter. At the least, it must be seen as a stratification system involving: (1) differential access to and control over resources; (2) differential exercise of power; and (3) an elaborate symbolic-ideological system that rationalizes and upholds the socio-economic system.[49]

In textbooks of sociology, class societies are contrasted with caste and estate societies. In the Marxian scheme, all societies based on antagonistic production relations are class societies, and clearly these include caste and estate societies. Both caste and estate presuppose the existence of a production system that enables the extraction of a surplus from the working population by a privileged class of upper castes, nobles, and rulers. Looked at from this perspective, caste must be seen as the concrete historical form in which class relations manifested themselves in India. This point of view seems to receive support from Godelier's analysis of kinship:

> In an archaic society kinship relations *function* as relations of production, just as they function as political relations. To use Marx's vocabulary kinship relations are here *both* infrastructure and superstructure. . . . To the extent that kinship in this kind of society really functions as relations of production, the determinant role of the economy does not contradict the dominant role of kinship, but is expressed through it.[50]

However, social structures are historical, and new conditions of production result in changes in existing class structure. There is little doubt that Indian society, particularly in Kuttanad, has passed through a period of unprecedented change during the past one hundred years in which capitalism and market relations have led to the development of internal class divisions within given castes themselves. Hence, the caste system today can no longer be regarded simply as a system of production relations. The exact nature of the concrete relationship between caste and class can be determined only by empirical investigation. Similarly, the question of how and to what extent caste has helped or hindered the development of class consciousness must also be regarded as an empirical question.

FIELDWORK AND COLLECTION OF DATA

Fieldwork for the study was conducted in India from September 1974 to September 1975. The first two months were spent in Delhi and Trivandrum, the national and state capital respectively, where library research was carried out and discussions were held with social scientists and other members of the local intelligentsia. From the middle of November until September 1975 the base for fieldwork was the town of Alleppey, the headquarters of the district bordering the Kuttanad region. The choice to settle in Alleppey was based mainly on considerations of convenience. Besides its obvious advantages for accommodation and other facilities, Alleppey offered a centre from where most of the important areas of Kuttanad were accessible by bus or boat. It also housed most of the offices of the government as well as those of the various organizations of the agricultural labourers and farmers of Kuttanad.

The study of Kuttanad poses some problems since it is neither coterminous with any revenue division nor a well-defined geographical area. For purposes of this study Kuttanad means the area under the jurisdiction of the Punja Special Office in Alleppey, comprising 10 revenue *taluks* of which 7 fall in Alleppey district and 3 in Kottayam district. Investigations were confined mainly to the 7 taluks in Alleppey district. All the areas of these 7 taluks do not lie in Kuttanad, however. While there are a total of 99 villages in the 7 taluks of Alleppey district, only 52 of these come within the area of Kuttanad. The only taluk whose entire area (12 villages) is included in Kuttanad is known by the same name (Kuttanad taluk) and can be said to constitute the central part of the region. The village survey which formed part of this study was conducted in this taluk.

The methods used to collect the data were those that best suited the objectives of the study. Since the aim was to gather as much information as possible on the social structure and the dynamics of social conflict and social change in Kuttanad, it was not deemed advisable to place any methodological restrictions on the inquiry. A combination of secondary research, quasi-participant observation, interviews, content analysis of local writings in both English and Malayalam, and a village survey became the source of data. The most important of these were, perhaps, the relatively lengthy and somewhat unstructured interviews with government officials, leaders and organizers of agricultural labour unions and farmers' associations, as well as with selected farmers and agricultural labourers. In all, seventy such interviews were conducted. Given the vastness of the region and its scanty transportation and communication facilities, this was by no means a mean achievement. Although many respondents could be reached in Alleppey, others had to be interviewed in their residences in various parts of Kuttanad. Often several trips had to be made to a respondent's office or residence before an interview could be held or completed. About one-third of the interviews were recorded on tapes; for the others notes were made which were often completed later in the evenings. Needless to say, there are limitations to a one-man study of this kind, and no claims are made that it is exhaustive or conclusive in any sense.

Because the intent was to gain an understanding of the development of class, class consciousness, and conflict in Kuttanad, and because of the limitations of time and resources, emphasis was placed on collecting historical and qualitative rather than quantitative and statistical data. However, the lack of primary quantitative data has been compensated for, in part, by extensive use of Census and other secondary data. Of course, it would have been preferable to have obtained more exact and detailed data on such aspects of the social structure as the distribution of castes.[51]

The period of fieldwork was a time when the political climate of Kuttanad had become relatively peaceful and calm after a period of intense and violent conflict. As we shall see later, the main reason for this calm was a new spirit of understanding and collaboration between the Communist Party of India (Marxist) and the Kerala Congress, and consequently of the two organizations of class enemies under their auspices, those of the agricultural labourers and the farmers. Elections were due in a year, and leaders of the two parties were engaged in intense manoeuvring to form a united front with a view to ousting the Communist Party of India (CPI) and its allies from power. Therefore, there was no evidence of political struggle apart from some largely ineffective excess-land campaigns and a few sporadic outbursts. On the other hand, the peaceful atmosphere may have facilitated fieldwork.

Establishing rapport with all the sections of the people, particularly with cadres of conflicting parties and organizations, is never an easy task. As I felt that from the beginning my own sympathies were with the agricultural labourers and their movement, I approached my fieldwork with some degree of caution, attempting as much as possible to establish rapport with the two sections of the population. As it happened, the leaders of the farmers' organizations and the Kerala Congress seemed more accessible and less suspicious or secretive than those of the labourers, who were also in most cases leaders of the CPI(M). This seems to have been the result, in part, of some basic differences between the two classes and their parties, the CPI(M) being far more ideologically oriented, close-knit, disciplined, and secretive.[52] It also seems possible that being a native of Kerala, I was assigned a particular caste and class position (my name indicated I was Syrian Christian and residence in Canada was taken to indicate relatively higher class status) with the result that the largely Syrian Christian farmers and Kerala Congress leaders were more favourably disposed towards me. Of course, the labourers themselves were friendly, co-operative, and open, to some extent more so than the farmers, who had often a few things to hide. In general, all the informants spoke openly and without reservations, although a certain amount of exaggeration and distortion had to be expected. The CPI(M) leaders, for instance, tended to play down the early role of many important leaders who were presently affiliated with the CPI—a practice of which their counterparts in the CPI were by no means innocent. Gathering information from the point of view of many parties and cross-checking them, in most cases several times, has helped to reconstruct events more or less as they occurred and to attain a high degree of reliability.

2

Agriculture in Kuttanad

Kuttanad is a low-lying, backwater region on the southwest coast of Kerala. Alleppey, an important commercial and industrial town in the old princely state of Travancore and now the headquarters of the new Alleppey district, lies on its western fringe; on the east it is bordered by Kottayam and Changanacherry, both important commercial towns. A narrow coastal strip of land on the western side of Kuttanad separates most of the region from the Arabian sea. The National Highway 47 runs along this coastal strip. The Vembanad *kayal* (lake), which starts as a narrow strip from the Arabian sea at Cochin, widens in area as it extends south and spreads into the northern half of Kuttanad. Four important rivers of Kerala—the Pumba, Manimala, Meenachil, and Achankoil—enrich Kuttanad's fields by depositing their silt as they crisscross into a large number of branches in the Kuttanad basin before discharging their water into the Vembanad lake. These rivers, together with the numerous man-made canals and the lake, make up a vast network of waterways throughout the entire region and provide the basis for its famed water transport system.

As noted before, Kuttanad is not coterminous with any revenue division. It comprises a total of 76 revenue villages of which 52 lie in Alleppey district and 24 in Kottayam district. The 76 villages fall in 10 taluks, 7 in Alleppey and 3 in Kottayam. With 52 out of 99 villages of Alleppey district falling in the region, Kuttanad constitutes a significant portion of the rural area of the district. As we shall see later, the proximity of Alleppey town has significantly affected economic, social, and political developments in the region. The total area of Kuttanad is estimated to be 1,642.2 km² out of which 1,439.1 km² are cultivable.[1]

However, as one of the two important "rice bowls" of Kerala, its economic importance far exceeds its size. Rice is the staple food of Kerala's 22 million people, but the state is able to produce only a little more than half its requirements. Of the total area under cultivation in the state, only about 35 per cent is available for paddy cultivation; more than half of the agricultural area is used up for the cultivation of cash crops such as rubber, tea, and coconuts.

Being water-logged, Kuttanad has few roads suitable for motor traffic, especially in its central regions. There are two roads that pass through the heart of Kuttanad from west to east. One of them is the recently constructed Alleppey-Changanacherry road which still has three unbridged large rivers across which government-financed free ferry service is now available. However, Kuttanad has a well-developed water transportation system; its waterways connect not only all the important cities and towns on its fringes—Cochin, Kottayam, Changanacherry, Alleppey, and Quilon—but also every town and village within the region. A traffic census taken in the mid-1950's showed that on an average 61 motor boats, 13 petrol barges, 8 tugs, and several hundred country boats passed through the Thanneermukom strait alone in the course of one day, and an estimated 9,680 persons and 9,280 tons of goods passed through Kuttanad's waterways daily.[2] Motor boats operated by the Kerala State Water Transport Corporation regularly pass through almost every village in the region. Many rich men own their own motor boats; many more people with less means own country boats and small canoes.

DEMOGRAPHIC AND SOCIO-ECONOMIC BACKGROUND

Kuttanad is a densely populated area. Its estimated population for 1971 is 1,698,000, which works out to an average of 1,021.6 persons per km^2 as against the Kerala average of 549 and the all-India average of 182.[3] Kuttanad's population density is almost two times that of Kerala, and Kerala itself occupies the first place among India's states in this respect. Thus it can be seen that Kuttanad is perhaps the most thickly populated region in the entire country. The population of Alleppey district, like that of Kerala, has grown at a very rapid rate. Between 1901 and 1971 it tripled, having increased by 310 per cent (see Table 1). It must, however, be noted that there has been a fall in the birth rate of Kerala and even more so of Alleppey district.[4] Between 1931 and 1972 Kerala's birth rate fell from 40 per 1,000 to 32.1 per 1,000 while the birth rate of all India fell from 45.2 to 38.4 during the same period. However, since the death rate in Kerala has fallen significantly to half that of all India, this has not had any significant effect on its rate of population growth.[5] Nevertheless, the decennial growth rate for Alleppey district alone between 1961 and 1971 has been only 17.73, as compared to 26.3 for Kerala.[16] The rate of growth for the previous decade was 19.03 per cent. Although figures were not available to substantiate it, it seems that family planning programmes are having some success in Kerala and in Alleppey in particular.

The man-land ratio in Alleppey district is one of the lowest in the state, and the per capita land available in the district is only 0.088 hectares, as compared with 0.224 hectares in Kerala. Despite the fact that Kuttanad is almost completely rural, the per capita land available in the region is only 0.095 hectares and of cultivable land even less (0.084 hectares). There is little scope for bringing any new land under cultivation since the area is already credited with the highest rate of land utilization in the state. However, further reclamation of some limited land from the lake remains a possibility.

Yet, this huge population concentrated in such a small patch of land is almost entirely dependent on agriculture for its livelihood. As may be expected, this region has one of the highest unemployment rates in the state. According to the estimates prepared by the Kuttanad Inquiry Commission on the basis of census figures of 1961 and 1971, only 469,000 persons, or 27.6 per cent of the total population of Kuttanad, are in the labour force, the rest of the population being dependent on them for their livelihood. This compares with a labour participation rate of 28.9 per cent for the state as a whole, showing a relatively greater burden of dependency per worker in Kuttanad. It may be noted that the labour participation rates for both Alleppey and Kerala have been steadily declining since 1901 (see Table 2). As we shall see later, this clearly reflects increasing unemployment and underemployment and perhaps also changes in age composition. Of those in the labour force 64.4 per cent are employed in agriculture as compared with 48.5 per cent for Kerala as a whole. The breakdown of this population into cultivators and agricultural labourers is given in Tables 3 and 4. These figures give an indication of the acute nature of the agrarian problem in Kuttanad. Agricultural labour makes up 69.5 per cent of those engaged in agriculture and 44 per cent of the entire work force in Kuttanad. For some areas in the central regions of Kuttanad the situation is even more acute. Thus in Kuttanad taluk, 70 per cent of the labour force is engaged in agriculture, and as much as 86 per cent of this is agricultural labour. Looked at from a different perspective, agricultural labour makes up 60 per cent of the total labour force in the taluk. This compares with 31 per cent for all Kerala.

The economic conditions of Kuttanad cannot be adequately described in isolation from those of the larger area of which it is a part, in particular Alleppey district. Given the great pressure on land one may expect that at least some portion of the labour force would be pushed out of agriculture and would be absorbed in the industries of the surrounding towns, especially Alleppey. But as the agrarian crisis has deepened in Kuttanad, the surrounding region, particularly Alleppey, has passed through what may be described as a process of deindustrialization. Once known as the Venice of India, Alleppey was the principal commercial and industrial town of the relatively prosperous princely state of Travancore. Alleppey's economic importance and prosperity rested on its coir industry, its oil mills, and its port. All three have been steadily declining during the postwar period. Its coir industry, which once produced the largest exports of the state, has almost collapsed; its oil mills have gone elsewhere, especially to Bombay, which has among other things more modern technology and more efficient machinery; its port has substantially declined in importance and has been replaced at least in part by the bigger port at Cochin, which is also the site of a new shipbuilding industry. Some smaller industries such as cashewnut processing have also declined during this period. The most damaging of all these changes has been the decline and near collapse of the coir industry.

TABLE 1: POPULATION DENSITY FOR ALLEPPEY DISTRICT, KERALA, INDIA, 1901-1971

(persons per km^2)

Census Year	Alleppey District	Kerala	India
1901	354	165	74
1911	406	184	79
1921	481	201	79
1931	598	245	91
1941	674	284	100
1951	805	345	113
1961	958	435	138
1971	1,128	549	182

Sources: *District Census Handbook, Alleppey,* 1971, p. 41; S. Krishna, Aiyer, *Keralathinte Sambadvyavastha* (Kerala: Bhasha Institute, 1975), p. 36.

TABLE 2: WORK PARTICIPATION RATE FOR KERALA, ALLEPPEY, AND KUTTANAD, 1901-1971

(per cent of total population)

Year	Kerala	Alleppey	Kuttanad
1901	44	—	—
1941	37	—	—
1961	33	33.7	—
1971	29.1	28.1	27.6

Sources: S. Krishna Aiyer, *Keralathinte Sambadvyavastha,* p. 41; *District Census Handbook, Alleppey,* 1971, p. 50.

TABLE 3: WORK PARTICIPATION BY AGRICULTURAL AND NON-AGRICULTURAL
CATEGORIES FOR KUTTANAD, ALLEPPEY, AND KERALA, 1971

Area	Total Workers	Workers in Agriculture	Workers in Non-Agricultural Occupations	Percentage of Workers in Agriculture to Total
Kuttanad	469,000	302,000*	167,000*	64.4
Alleppey	598,468	279,279	319,189	46.7
Kerala	6,216,459	3,014,777	3,201,582	48.5

*These figures have been computed from the 1961 census data in conjunction
with certain broad totals from 1971 census.

Sources: Compiled from figures in the *Report of the Kuttanad Inquiry Commission,* p. 7; *District Census Handbook, Alleppey,* p. 51; Aiyer, *Keralathinte Sambadvyavastha,* p. 43.

TABLE 4: PERCENTAGE DISTRIBUTION OF THE LABOUR FORCE ENGAGED IN
AGRICULTURE IN KUTTANAD, ALLEPPEY, AND KERALA, 1971

Area	Kuttanad	Alleppey District	Kerala
Total Workers in Agriculture	100.0	100.0	100.0
Cultivators	30.46	34.3	36.7
Agricultural Labourers	69.54	65.7	63.3

Sources: *Report of the Kuttanad Inquiry Commission,* p. 7; *District Census Handbook, Alleppey,* p. 51; Aiyer, *Keralathinte Sambadvyavastha,* p. 43.

The coir industry in Alleppey is more than a hundred years old; the first coir factory there was built in 1859 by an Englishman from Calcutta where he had already seen manually manufactured coir yarn from Alleppey.[7] The principal raw material for the industry is coconut husk, which is abundant in Alleppey and the surrounding areas. As the industry expanded, labourers were recruited from the rural areas near Alleppey. During the period between the two wars branch factories, as well as small independent factories, sprang up all along the coastal strip of the backwater area. Between 1932 and 1937 Travancore exported more than 10 million rupees' worth of coir goods annually. In 1939 there were a total of 290 factories in Alleppey and the surrounding regions, and Alleppey town still housed the main factories and offices of nearly all the big manufacturers. In 1939 a board of conciliation of trade disputes appointed by the Travancore government estimated that there were about 27,000 workers employed in the coir factories of the state and that about 18,000 families were supported by the industry.[8] It must also be noted that many tasks such as the soaking and preparation of husks were done mostly at home and only the manufacture of mats and matting was carried out in the factories. Hence, there were always more workers employed in the coir cottage industries than in the factories themselves.

We have no exact and reliable data on the extent of the decline of the coir industry or of the unemployment caused by it. According to the Techno-Economic Survey of Kerala, Travancore as a whole had 144 coir factories in 1951, but only 124 factories in 1959.[9] And in all of Kerala there were 16,075 coir workers in 1951, but only 12,343 workers in 1959.[10] There is no record of industrial manpower available for Alleppey district. According to information gathered from various knowledgeable persons in Alleppey, the industry began declining around 1946 after having enjoyed a short-lived boom during the war. By the early 1960's factories began to close down on a massive scale. The district labour officer estimates that in Alleppey alone at least 45,000 workers lost their jobs, jeopardizing the livelihood of their families. Some of them seem to have found employment in the ''feeder factories'' subsequently started by the former factory employees either as co-operative ventures or as individual enterprises.[11] These factories are kept small, a typical one employing only about 5 to 7 persons and manufacturing coir products to be sold to merchant exporters. By keeping these factories small the employers can escape the provisions of the Factories Act and keep the workers ''under control.'' It is estimated that at present there are nearly 2,000 such factories in operation in and around Alleppey town. Those workers who have managed to find employment in these factories appear to have suffered not only a substantial decline in their wages but also job insecurity, as well as the loss of fringe benefits such as bonuses, Employees' State Insurance, and provident funds.[12]

While it is difficult to provide an adequate explanation for the decline of the coir industry, it is interesting to note that many upper-class persons, particularly landowners in Kuttanad, attributed it to the unrest and ''lawlessness'' unleashed by the coir workers and their Communist-dominated union. The decline in the coir industry was caused by many factors, economic and political, some of which had their source outside Alleppey and Kerala, and even India. The collapse of the United Kingdom and western European markets and competition from synthetic products seem to have had disastrous effects on the industry. In recent years the Kerala government has been making at least some feeble efforts to revive the industry. It has managed to maintain a static export level of Rs.150 million a year, three-fourths of which is now absorbed by the East European countries.[13] The government has also taken the initiative in establishing a glass factory and a pharmaceuticals factory, both near Alleppey. But Alleppey does not seem to be recovering. Today, it strikes a visitor as a dying town, with its closed factories, its stinking and mosquito-emitting canals, and its dilapidated hotels and office buildings.

Although it is difficult to assess the impact of the deindustrialization of Alleppey on Kuttanad and its agriculture, there is little doubt that it has greatly contributed to the pressure on the land. The Kuttanad region had been an important supplier of the labour force for the coir industry. Now, increasingly, its labour force is compelled to fall back on agriculture for its livelihood.

LITERACY AND EDUCATION

There are few rural areas in the entire country with a literacy rate as high as that of Kuttanad. Travancore had long been a leader in education and social and cultural advancement and had come to be called a model state. Today, Kerala has the highest literacy rate for any state in India, and within Kerala, Alleppey district occupies the first place in this respect. Table 5 compares Kuttanad's literacy with that of Alleppey district, Kerala, and India, respectively. Table 6 provides a breakdown of the literacy rate of Alleppey district by sex. It can be seen that although women trail behind men, the female literacy rate is nevertheless remarkably high in the area. It is also worth noting, as is evident from Table 7, that there are no significant rural-urban differences with regard to literacy. In fact, in the case of females the rural rate was slightly higher in 1971. This reflects a feature that is common to the whole of Kerala—a general absence of any sharp rural-urban differences and the intense interaction between rural and urban communities. This may be partly due to the fact that Kerala has no large urban centre worth its name. The relatively high rates of literacy and education are seen in the attitudes and practices of the people. I have already referred to the acceptance of the family-planning programme by at least some sections of the population. A shopkeeper in Alleppey told me that now it was not uncommon to find young women buying family-planning devices openly from the shops—something that would be considered shocking in most other parts of India.

TABLE 5: LITERACY RATES FOR KUTTANAD, ALLEPPEY, KERALA, AND INDIA, 1961 AND 1971

Year	Kuttanad	Alleppey District	Kerala	India
1961	—	56.90	46.8	23.7
1971	72	70.44	60.42	29.3

Sources: Census of India, 1971; *Report of the Kuttanad Inquiry Commission.*

TABLE 6: LITERACY RATES IN ALLEPPEY DISTRICT BY SEX, 1961 AND 1971

Year	Total	Male	Female
1961	56.90	63.84	50.15
1971	70.44	75.22	65.79

Source: *District Census Handbook, Alleppey,* p. 48.

TABLE 7: RURAL-URBAN LITERACY BY SEX, ALLEPPEY DISTRICT, 1971

Area	Total	Male	Female
Rural	70.50	75.22	65.92
Urban	70.15	75.27	65.14

Source: Adapted from figures in *District Census Handbook, Alleppey,* p. 48.

ECOLOGICAL FEATURES

The basic ecological datum about Kuttanad is that it is waterlogged; its paddy fields lie below mean sea level and are submerged under water during the greater part of the year. As a result, both human habitation and agriculture have been made possible only by a highly labour-intensive process of reclamations. An estimated 627.9 km² have been raised 1 to 2 metres above water level and converted into garden lands mainly used for human habitation and coconut cultivation. The remaining 811 km² is wet land in which paddy is cultivated.[14] Garden lands become more extensive as we approach the upper Kuttanad area, that is, the relatively shallow deltaic regions of the rivers. The area in and around the lake, where the water level is deeper, is known as lower Kuttanad. During the monsoon season the entire region is a vast sheet of water dotted with coconut groves near the houses of landowners and the tiny plots of land, also filled with coconut trees, which house the huts of the landless labourers. At this time, many houses, especially the homesteads of the landless labourers, are accessible only by boat. In fact, it is not uncommon to find a few homesteads partially submerged.

The paddy fields lie in blocks, known as *padasekharams,* which are encircled by protective ring *bunds* (dykes). These bunds were first erected when the fields were reclaimed, and they are repaired and renovated every crop season before water is pumped out and the fields recovered for cultivation. There are a total of 1,129 padasekharams in Kuttanad, ranging in size from 4 to 960 hectares. Of these 32 are *kayal*[15] *padasekharams* which have been reclaimed from the lake. These are of more recent origin, relatively extensive, and amount to roughly 14 per cent of the total area of padasekharams.[16] Being deeper, the kayal areas present greater problems in bunding and draining water. However, the difference between these and the remaining *karappadams* is only one of degree, since all paddy cultivation in Kuttanad requires bunding and draining operations. This system of cultivation is known as *punja* cultivation in Kerala.

THE RECLAMATIONS

The reclamations of land from the backwaters of Kuttanad have had a remarkable and unusual history. In the first place, they are among the few operations of their kind anywhere to be undertaken largely by relatively small cultivators with slender resources. Secondly, they have been accomplished with local materials, with little use of modern technology and machines, and with the abundant and intensive use of locally available human labour.[17] Of course, they have been done in patches and over a period of time. The "Old Reclamation" was confined to the shallow upper Kuttanad area; but exhaustion of that area, the pressure on land, and the possibility of making new profits attracted the more enterprising of Kuttanad's agricultural entrepreneurs to the "New Reclamations" in the Vembanad lake.

Although information is scanty about the history of these reclamations it seems certain that the process had begun at least by 1834.[18] It is significant that from 1886-87 on, the government of Travancore participated in this enterprise not only by undertaking some projects on its own, but more importantly by granting loans, subsidies, and tax exemptions to the private entrepreneurs.[19] In June 1888 the government set apart a sum of Rs. 50,000 to be advanced as loans to the *ryots* (cultivating tenants) for "reclaiming and bringing under cultivation portions of the Vembanad backwater along the shore within the taluks Amabalapuzha, Changanacherry, Kottayam, Ettumannoor, Vaikom and Shertallai."[20] An individual could receive a loan of up to Rs. 5,000 on 4 per cent interest per annum. It is interesting to note that the 1880's saw a surge of interest in land reclamation on the part of both the government and the private entrepreneurs. It is possible that this was a time of acute food shortage. In any case, the enterprise continued to attract many individuals from the important families of the area. The reclamations received a temporary setback between 1903 and 1912 when apprehension about their possible effects on the Cochin port led to the suspension of the activity by the Travancore government. But the reclamations continued unabated after that date and reached a peak in the late 1930's. It was in 1941 that the locally famous landlord and "kayal king" Murickan obtained the government's authorization to reclaim 3 blocks with a total of 581.6 hectares. The government was to receive a fixed price *(tharavila)* of Rs. 25 per hectare to be paid in 10 equal instalments. No tax would be levied for the first 2 years, after which full tax payments would have to be made. In all, this landlord, the biggest ever in Kuttanad, is said to have reclaimed over 936 hectares of land in 6 blocks. About 8,000 hectares of the Vambanad Lake alone had been brought under the plough by 1945. The last in the series of reclamations has been what is known as the 'R' block or 'Holland Project' of the early 1960's. This was a unique project in Kuttanad that converted an estimated 616 hectares of kayal into dry land. It is protected by permanent, non-submersible bunds standing at a height of 1.8 metres above mean sea level and with top width of 3 metres; it is served by 21 centrifugal pumps at suitable sites which bail out water on a permanent basis. Though this government-financed project was undertaken with a view to raising a second crop of paddy, this aim has been defeated by the private owners of the plots in the block who have opted in favour of more lucrative cash crops, such as coconuts and sugar cane.

The two most difficult and hazardous tasks in reclamation are bunding and draining water. The bunds had to be erected in water whose depth, in the kayal areas, ranged from 3 to 6 metres. They also had to be strong enough to withstand tidal action. Kuttanad's cultivators devised an ingenious method to achieve this task using only local material and local labour—a method that has not only withstood the test of time but has also been found more feasible than modern methods under some conditions.[21] Piles of coconut trunks are driven deep into the bed of the water around the proposed area in two lines, which are then fenced with bamboo screens on either side. The grove between the two lines is then filled with clay, sand, twigs, straw, and garbage of all kinds. Clay of the required consistency is gathered from the bed of the canals, rivers, or the Vembanad lake by the workers from a depth of 6 to 7.5 metres. The workers have to dive to the depths of the water to gather the clay with their bare hands, then transport it in manually rowed country boats to the site of the bund. Clad only in loincloths, they work in mud and water all day long. The last stage in the construction of the bunds is particularly difficult and risky, especially when the water level is deep and the current strong. As the two ends of the ring bund are joined, hundreds of men work together in a concerted and quick operation with sandbags, wooden poles, and other necessary material. It is said that in the past a Pulaya worker was sacrificed and buried alive under this portion of the bund in order to appease the gods and to ensure that the bund remained firm.[22]

Unlike the construction of bunds, which is done only once at the time of first reclamation (although bunds are kept repaired and renovated year after year), the draining of water is a task that must be performed anew every crop season. In the past it was an arduous and time-consuming task, as the only device available was the hand-operated water wheel; innovations in technology for the control of water have been crucial in the development of agriculture in Kuttanad. It appears that punja cultivation in Kuttanad remained at a subsistence level well into the early years of this century. Paddy was cultivated in the shallower areas of Kuttanad once in 2 or 3 years, and since the rivers deposited enough silt by this time the cultivator seldom manured his fields. The introduction of the pumping engine in 1912 seems to have revolutionized paddy cultivation in Kuttanad. The replacement of oil with electric engines later marked another stage in this process. It became possible to engage in large-scale commercial farming organized on a capitalist basis. Since 1916 the state government has undertaken a number of projects in Kuttanad for the control and proper utilization of its water resources. These include the construction of the Thottappally spillway in 1955 to discharge surplus flood water into the sea, the construction of the Thanneermukkam Salt Water Barrier to prevent the intrusion of salt water into Kuttanad when the water level in its rivers is low in the summer, and the establishment of the Punja Special Office in Alleppey in 1941 which, among other things, supervises and subsidizes draining operations in Kuttanad. The Kuttanad Development Scheme, now in progress, is expected to convert 52,000 hectares of single-crop paddy fields into double-crop fields through the use of permanent bunds.

AGRICULTURAL OPERATIONS

The problem faced by the Kuttanad cultivator is to keep his fields protected from the vagaries of nature for a period long enough to grow his crop. By proper timing of the cropping period most farmers now raise a single crop between September to October and January to February, thus avoiding the southwest monsoon floods (June to August) and the advent of saline water (February to March). In some parts of upper Kuttanad a second crop has been traditionally cultivated using a deep-water variety of paddy called *kolappala,* which matures in September with the ear heads floating on the surface of the water and is harvested, bundled up, and transported in small canoes. More recently, a second crop has been attempted on a little more extensive scale. This is, however, recognized as a gamble and is successful only if nature is kind and keeps the fields free from floods as well as salinity. It is now hoped that with the completion of the Kuttanad Development Project two crops can be raised in most of the paddy fields of Kuttanad.

Preparations for the main (punja) crop begin in January or February immediately after harvesting the previous crop. After one round of dry ploughing, lime is applied to the soil to neutralize its acidity; the fields are then flooded by opening the sluices in the bunds, and left to remain submerged throughout the southwest monsoon period. By July to August the water in the lake and the rivers begins to recede, and at this time a second round of ploughing (wet ploughing) is undertaken. This is a difficult and unpleasant operation which requires the workers to wade through waist-deep and muddy water with their draught animals and ploughs. Cattle and buffalo are used as draught animals; during the ploughing season many are brought from outside Kuttanad to meet the increased demand. When the water level reaches manageable levels the ring bunds protecting the padasekharams are repaired. After the outer bunds are completely repaired, excess water is pumped out from the fields by means of electric, or sometimes oil, engines. Drainage operations are carried out on a large scale, covering a whole padasekharam at a time, and are done through the Punja Special Office, which gives the job to private contractors through auction. Part of the expenditure for this operation is borne by the government in the form of a subsidy to the farmers. Drainage operations usually continue uninterrupted for three to four weeks, at the end of which the farmers begin repairing the inner bunds that demarcate the individual plots within a padasekharam. The irrigation channels are also repaired. The soil is then raked slightly with a harrow. After this the women workers enter the fields to carry out a first round of weeding and to work the soil into a soft puddle. Fresh water is then let into the fields to a depth of up to 25 centimetres, depending on the lay of the land.

When the preparations have thus been completed and the fields are ready, sprouted seeds are sown in knee-deep water. In most parts of Kuttanad sowing is done by broadcasting, although transplanting is also practised in some limited areas. The rationale for this appears to be the dearth of land for nurseries. There are a number of operations that are carried out between the time of sowing and that of harvesting. These include further weeding, the application of fertilizers, and the spraying of pesticides. With the use of high-yielding varieties of seeds, fertilizers are generally applied twice and pesticides sprayed three to four times a season. Fresh water is let in and pumped out several times until the grain setting stage (about fifteen days after flowering), after which the fields are allowed to dry in preparation for the harvest. Harvesting is done in January or February. The wages for harvesting are paid in kind and are generally considered lucrative. The harvesting is done by most cultivators around the same time and it attracts a large number of migrant workers from various places around Kuttanad, particularly from the depressed coastal areas north of Alleppey. These people can be found camping at various points in Kuttanad with their pans, pots, and mats till the end of the harvest season.

It can be seen that paddy cultivation in Kuttanad is very risky and requires a series of extremely labour-intensive operations at decisive periods during the crop season. Paddy growing a metre or more below water level and separated from water only by the crudely made ring bund can hardly be considered secure. Breaches in the bund can and do cause havoc to the crop and leave the cultivator bankrupt for the year. Such a disaster can be prevented only by keeping vigil, especially during the monsoons. If and when breaches do occur they must be repaired immediately. Proper timing is crucial to many operations, such as sowing, weeding, ploughing, and harvesting; postponement for even a few days can jeopardize the crop. It can be seen that the threat of a strike at these points can be very effective and give tremendous bargaining power to the workers. Furthermore, since the operations are labour-intensive and performed on a large scale, they bring hundreds of workers together to the fields to work under the supervision of the landowners or the managers appointed by them. In certain respects, the paddy field in Kuttanad resembles an assembly line rather than a farm, and the farmers of Kuttanad resemble, both in their lifestyle and attitudes, a commercial class rather than a peasantry. These features, as will be seen, have been favourable to the organization of labour.

THE GREEN REVOLUTION

The Green Revolution package was introduced under the auspices of the Ford Foundation and the United States government into different parts of the world about the same time and has produced fairly similar results.[23] India, which had passed through a period of serious food shortages and had become dependent on Western countries to feed its population, was to be an important experimental ground for the package. Its strategy called for the injection of new high-yielding variety seeds (HYV's) and high-energy technology (chemical fertilizers, pumpsets, pesticides, tractors) in selected, favourable areas without any attempt to change the agrarian structure. This means that government subsidization of the rich landowners was to be an important feature of the programme.

In 1962-63 Alleppey and Palghat districts in Kerala were chosen to come under the Intensive Agricultural District Programme (IADP). It appears that two districts were chosen in Kerala as against one in other states primarily because of their considerably smaller size. Except for the Mandhya district in Mysore, every other IADP district had an area larger than the combined area of Alleppey and Palghat together.[24] It is significant to note that these are the two "rice bowls" of Kerala and that the programme in Kerala concentrated mainly on paddy production. It seems certain that paddy cultivation in Kuttanad was fairly advanced even before the advent of the programme and that its relatively progressive farmers had already been using such improved strains of paddy as PTB and C.O.25. The existence of the rice research station at the heart of Kuttanad at Mankompu and its work with some improved strains had created a certain amount of willingness and enthusiasm among the farmers to experiment with new varieties of seed. It is therefore difficult to assess exactly the extent to which the programme has been directly responsible for the changes in the patterns of paddy cultivation in Kuttanad. Surprisingly, many farmers were, when asked, only vaguely aware of the existence of the programme although they had been using HYVs, chemical fertilizers, and pesticides for several years.

Although new varieties of paddy were introduced into Kuttanad in 1966, their real adoption can be said to have begun on a significant scale only with the widespread use of IR8 in 1967-68.[25] The results were very encouraging though short-lived. Since then a large number of high-yielding varieties have been introduced, and their reception has been very quick and widespread. The amount of land under cultivation with the new varieties grew rapidly, and today it is the rare farmer in Kuttanad who is still using the traditional local variety. Chemical fertilizers and pesticides have also been adopted very widely and on a relatively large scale. Since fertilizers are an essential component of the Green Revolution package, these were provided at subsidized rates in Alleppey district. The number of fertilizer depots in Alleppey district increased from 249 in 1961-62 to 403 in 1969-70. It is estimated that the per hectare consumption of fertilizers has increased from 61 kg in 1961-62 to 190 kg in 1968-69. This represents an annual growth rate of 30 per cent as against 14 per cent in the developing countries.[26] Pesticides are also part of the package and have been widely adopted. Moreover, it has now become evident that the new varieties and the vastly increased use of fertilizers have themselves contributed greatly to the vulnerability of paddy to pests and diseases. The brown hopper, in particular, is becoming an increasing menace to paddy cultivation in Kuttanad. Several informants reported that the old local variety of paddy was resistant to brown hopper, which began to make its menacing appearance only with the introduction of the new varieties. This has compelled them to use pesticides more frequently and in greater quantity. After 1970, however, the enormous rise in the cost of the pesticide seems to have made them more sparing and calculating in its use. In any case, they believe that there can be no going back to the old local variety.

In general, the performance of IADP in Alleppey district has been considered disappointing. According to an evaluation report of the Kerala State Planning Board, during the 9 year period ending in 1969-70 production of paddy in Alleppey district increased by only 15 per cent, while it increased by 27 per cent in Palghat district during the same period.[27] And in a study based on data drawn from the bureau of Economics and Statistics Oommen states that ''in terms of both the area under new varieties of rice and the productivity of rice, the situation in Alleppey district compares unfavourably with Kerala as a whole.''[28] Furthermore, even this marginal increase in total production is attributed to the increase in area under cultivation.[29] While all this may be true, the evaluation report also draws attention to another fact: in the package districts some limited areas with special potentialities, in particular, the Palghat taluk of Palghat district and the Kuttanad region of Alleppey district, registered substantial increase in production. The mean yield of paddy in the Kuttanad region rose to 3,378 kg per hectare in 1968-69, against the mean yield of 2,262 kg per hectare for the district as a whole. In 1969-70 the region registered even further increase in productivity.[30] If we consider Kuttanad taluk alone it can be seen that paddy production increased by 152.3 per cent between 1958-59 and 1969-70.[31] It seems that the average for the district as a whole was considerably brought down by the sub-marginal coastal belt and Onattukara region where productivity remained at a low level.[32]

Evidence collected during the present study confirms this trend and suggests that the increase in the productivity of paddy in Kuttanad has been considerable, although the Green Revolution may have created its own new problems. There was widespread agreement among informants that with the use of the new varieties the yield has gone up from 250-375 *paras*[33] per hectare to 625-750 paras per hectare—an increase of at least 100 per cent. Many informants were farmers who, as a rule, attempted to hide their successes and profits and to exaggerate their expenses and losses. Visits to farms during harvests verified the accuracy of these figures. During 1974-75 a few instances of yields up to 875 paras per hectare in the kayal areas were observed. On the other hand, an occasional crop that had been seriously damaged either by saline water or by brown hopper would yield only 375 paras per hectare. On the basis of the reports of the farmers visited, the average was 675 paras per hectare. It must be noted, however, that this particular harvest season was a good one, and both the natural hazards of paddy cultivation in Kuttanad and the relatively higher risks involved in the cultivation of the new varieties of seed were absent that year. Given the unpredictable and erratic pattern of yields in Kuttanad, it seems likely that the average yields would work out to be less than the 675 paras per hectare over a period of a few years. Nevertheless, it is noteworthy that labour unrest in Kuttanad seems to have had little or no adverse effect on productivity.

There is little doubt that paddy cultivation in Kuttanad has become a much more lucrative enterprise than before, although it still remains risky and requires much more capital and more skillful operations. During 1974-75 when the price of paddy went up to Rs. 14 per para a Kuttanad farmer could make a profit of Rs. 3,500 or more per hectare. It was not uncommon in Kuttanad for a relatively large landowner to make a profit of Rs. 100,000 or more from the first crop alone, having additional income from his coconut gardens, from a second crop, and from other investments.

The Green Revolution has further accentuated the capitalist nature of farming in Kuttanad. Paddy cultivation, in particular, is now a lucrative, albeit risky, enterprise which requires huge investments and the employment at decisive stages during the crop season of a large labour force. A Kuttanad farmer who cultivates 40 hectares of paddy fields must invest a sum of Rs. 175,000 each crop season in order to make a profit of Rs. 100,000 or more. Some of the implications of these developments for agrarian relations in Kuttanad will be analyzed later.

3

Agrarian Relations in Kuttanad

While Nature has been bountiful to the inhabitants of Kuttanad, their own input in the form of intense human labour and constant vigilance has been crucial in the development of its agriculture. "God created the earth and the waters," said an old Nair politician from Kuttanad, "but the people created Kuttanad by raising it from the waters." It hardly needs be said, however, that all the inhabitants of this land did not and do not share equally either the back-breaking toil or the fruits that are reaped from it. A complex division of labour, based on the caste system and differential rights and duties in relation to land and labour, developed in Kuttanad quite early. This enabled various privileged strata in society to extract the surplus produced by the actual tillers of the land. The complexity of this system and the problems facing the sociologist in attempting to represent and explain it adequately have already been discussed. What is important to note here is that at least during the last few hundred years a clear relationship has existed among caste, landownership, and the extent of participation in labour. Thus, for instance, the landless agricultural labourers of today are also in large part untouchables whose ancestors constituted the bulk of the actual tillers of the land before the abolition of slavery in 1855.

To discuss agrarian structure in Kuttanad it is necessary to place it in the context of the historical development of land and society in Travancore and, to some extent, in the whole of Kerala. While the agrarian history of Travancore shared many features with that of the rest of India, it also had some important differences. Ecological and political factors combined to keep Kerala isolated from the rest of the country and to develop an agrarian system that, in the view of some writers, resembled European feudalism in some important respects. Mencher, for instance, has drawn attention to the ways in which ecological conditions have influenced the formation of loosely organized and dispersed settlement patterns in Kerala which stand out in sharp contrast to the nuclear village settlements in other parts of India.[1] There is, she argues, a complex interrelationship between these settlement patterns, land tenure, the caste system, and authority relations:

> In Kerala, authority relations between higher and lower castes were always directed from a given unpartitioned upper-caste landlord family toward the families who either worked for them as tenant farmers, coolies or agrestic slaves, or with whom they maintained one or another category of service relationship. . . . On the whole, authority tended to run from the large landlord family to those under him, in a way reminiscent of the European feudal manor.[2]

In the same vein, Kerala's foremost Marxist theoretician, Namboothiripad, sees Kerala forming an exception to the Marxian model of Asiatic or Oriental society. The "material condition" of Kerala, he argues, is unique because, unlike in other parts of India, field cultivation there does not require canal irrigation or other forms of public work:

> This distinctive feature of Kerala's material condition should be the starting point of any scientific study of Kerala's history. . . . The essence of this path of Kerala is the existence of landed property of feudalism, the absence of which has been noted by Marxists as the principal feature of Oriental Society.[3]

Perhaps as a result of these factors and the barrier provided by the Western Ghats, Kerala remained politically isolated during much of its history, divided into tiny principalities and ruled by petty chieftains who commanded their own armies. Most attempts to bring Kerala under any central administration met with little success. It was only towards the end of the eighteenth century that the Raja Marthanda Varma completed his ambitious programme of conquering his neighbouring chieftains to establish the state of Travancore. One of these conquered principalities was Chempakacherry, whose territory consisted mostly of present-day Kuttanad. The Raja of Travancore followed a policy of suppressing the power of the chieftains by annexing their lands and turning them into state property. Thus the state emerged as the super landlord in Travancore. This process continued unabated, and by the beginning of the twentieth century 86 per cent of the total cultivated land and 80 per cent of the total cultivated wet land had come under the ownership of the state. The remaining portion was in the hands of private owners, known in Kerala as *janmies*. It should be noted that as far as *janmom* lands were concerned, the superior castes had a monopoly of ownership. The *circar* or government lands were leased out to tenant cultivators relatively more freely, although here again caste seems to have played an important role. There developed, of course, a variety of subtenancies, increasingly so as time went on, which could be given to relatively lower castes in the middle ranges of the hierarchy.[4]

The Travancore government also took some pioneering steps in the direction of land reforms. In 1865 it made the historic *pattom* proclamation conferring full ownership rights to the pattom tenants of circar lands who formed the bulk of the tenants of the state. The tenants also became free to transfer their lands. As a result of this, land became a commodity in the market, and within one year following the declaration land valued at about Rs. 475,000 was sold among the cultivators.[5] It may be of interest here to note that this period saw a sudden spurt in the reclamation of waste lands in the backwater area of Kuttanad. The government also took some measures in improving the status of the tenants of janmom lands. Among the several measures the one that stands out is the royal proclamation as amended in 1933 which conferred occupancy rights on them except for non-payment of *janmi karom*, or rent, to the janmies.

These developments placed the cultivators of Travancore in a favoured position in relation to their counterparts in British India, particularly in Malabar whose misery and insecurity under a very oppressive land tenure system are well known. However, they did not spell the end of landlordism or pave the way for the emergence of independent peasant cultivators generally. Such a tendency was arrested and even reversed, at least partly, as new land leasing began to develop with a variety of tenurial rights. The new forms of landlordism and the number of new intermediaries increased greatly during the first half of the twentieth century.[6] Nevertheless, land sales became widespread, land values increased, and a class of independent cultivators emerged; all these seem to have expedited capitalist developments in agriculture.

Travancore also witnessed a great expansion in trade and commerce. By the end of the nineteenth century, agriculture had expanded greatly. The phenomenal increase in the price of agricultural products and the expansion of transport opened up new opportunities. British capital entered Travancore, mainly in the coir industry in the coastal areas around Alleppey and in the plantations of the eastern hill regions of the state. One local entrepreneurial caste that came forward to take advantage of these new opportunities was that of the Syrian Christians,[7] whose members had already been quietly investing in land capital made from trade and commerce. They also initiated the organization of indigenous credit institutions known as *kuris* and *chitties* which were the first mobilizers of local savings and capital. From the 1920's they were in the forefront of banking, which saw rapid growth during the next 15 years. Between 1925-26 and 1932-33 the number of banking, loan, and insurance companies in Travancore grew from 44 to 784, thereafter gradually declining to 163 in 1948-49.[8] It is of interest that these new banking institutions were concentrated mainly in those regions where agricultural development and growth were most prominent. This means that the development of banking and commerce were related to the development of capitalist agriculture, and that conversely, "the capitalist developments in agriculture . . . were intimately related to the expansion of credit."[9] The following observations made by the Travancore-Cochin Banking Inquiry Commission in 1956 are instructive:

> As a matter of fact, most of the banks in Travancore-Cochin state were initially started in what were mere hamlets such as Thiruvalla, Kottayam, Chengannoor, Kozhencherry, Thalavady, Palai, etc., which were not even municipal towns then. It was only later that these banks opened out branches in larger towns.[10]

It should be pointed out that the places mentioned here are all Syrian Christian strongholds and with the single exception of Palai lie in or on the fringes of Kuttanad. It is interesting that this period saw another spurt in reclamations in Kuttanad and in the extension of plantations in the hill regions of the state, although it seems likely that the Kuttanad reclamations may have also been helped by the black-market price of rice.[11]

CASTE, LAND, AND LABOUR

Swami Vivekanada is said to have referred to Kerala as the "madhouse of India" because of the rigidity with which it practised untouchability and the other social restrictions associated with the caste system. All the important castes in Kerala are found in Kuttanad: Brahmins, Nairs, Syrian Christians, Ezhavas, and Harijans.[12] Unfortunately, there is no caste breakdown of the population of Kuttanad. The 1961 Census gives a breakdown of the population of Alleppey district by religion. The two major religious groups are Hindus and Christians, with Hindus forming 65.5 per cent, Christians 28.5 per cent, and Muslims 6 per cent. The proportion of Christians is higher in the Kuttanad region than in Alleppey district as a whole. Their percentage in Kuttanad taluk is 44. It is important to point out, however, that the Christians, too, are differentiated among themselves both by class and by caste; the economically and politically dominant Syrian Christians who claim higher-caste descent are sharply differentiated from the economically depressed "neo-Christians" who are more recent converts from lower, especially untouchable, castes.[13] It is striking that in the context of class antagonism, political organization, and class struggle, these neo-Christians have stood solidly with their non-Christian class allies, caste men, and, in many cases, relatives in opposition to the landowning class, which in Kuttanad is predominantly Syrian Christian.

Traditionally, the caste owning most land in Kuttanad was the Brahmins, who also occupied the highest position in the caste hierarchy. Numerically, they never represented more than a tiny fraction of the population. A Namboothiri Brahmin *illom*[14] in Mamkompu in Kuttanad taluk, the *Kulangara Madhom*, at one time owned large tracts of land in the area which are now in the possession of their former tenants, some of them now among the wealthiest Syrian Christian families in Kuttanad. The locally dominant Namboothiri Brahmins were joined by a few Tamil Brahmin families who migrated to Kuttanad from Kumbakonam in Tamil Nadu about 350 years ago. The Tamil Brahmins soon became large landowners and moneylenders and are even today among the wealthiest families in Kuttanad. The decline of the Namboothiri Brahmins has been total;[15] the few Tamil Brahmin families, though wealthy, are a small minority, and Brahmins as a whole are not a significant part of the social and political scene in Kuttanad today.

The Nairs, who come next to the Brahmins in the caste hierarchy, have been an important group in Kuttanad. Traditionally they were a martial or military aristocracy who formed the Kerala equivalent of a Kshatriya caste. Almost all the rulers and chieftains in the various principalities of Kerala came from this caste. They were also large landlords and cultivators with superior tenancy rights and probably were the most important and powerful landowning group at the turn of the century. A number of aristocratic Nair families are found in Kuttanad even to this day.[16] However, the Nairs have also declined in power and wealth, although not to the same extent as the Namboothiris.[17] Unlike the Namboothiris they took an active interest in modern education and are found in large numbers in politics, industry, and in the modern professions. In Kuttanad the Nairs have lost a great deal of land during the last hundred years, and it is quite common to find impoverished Nair families who were in the recent past wealthy or at least relatively well off. Impoverished Nairs, like impoverished and dispossessed upper castes in general, have provided many recruits to radical parties in Kerala during the last four decades. In Kuttanad many Nairs have been among the leaders of the communist movement, but after the split in the Party, they have generally tended to support the Communist Party of India while the lower castes have predominantly been supporting the Communist Party of India (Marxist), locally known as the Marxist Party. Despite their losses, they are still a landowning caste and are second only to the Syrian Christians in power and wealth.

Of all the castes in Kuttanad, it was the Syrian Christians who benefitted most from the decline of the old landed aristocracies. Despite the fact that they always enjoyed a relatively high position in the social system, and have had among them a few landed aristocrats and wealthy traders, the vast majority of them were in the past cultivators of the lands of the Brahmin and Nair landlords and the large Nair tenants. As noted, in Travancore the Syrian Christians were among the early bearers of the protestant virtues and the capitalist ethos and played a pioneering role in banking and commerce. Given the high social status associated with land-ownership, it was only natural that they invested their profits in land. In Kuttanad they seem to have prospered also from paddy cultivation. They found that with frugal living, hard work, wise planning, and a few good crops they could become full owners of their own land. They gradually emerged as a leading landowning caste; an Economic Census taken in 1931 found that next to the Brahmins they were the biggest landowners in Travancore.[18] A substantial portion of the cultivated land in Kuttanad today is in their hands (see Table 8). Although full owner-ship rights were conferred on tenants only after the land reforms of 1964, a con-siderable amount of land had come under the ownership of the Syrian Christians even before that date. They seem to have benefitted greatly from the immense rise in the price of paddy during the years of the Second World War. There was yet another factor that may have helped the Syrian Christians in their rise to power. They were able to take advantage of the new educational opportunities offered in the state from the middle of the nineteenth century by missionaries and church-dominated institutions. It is interesting to observe that some of the earli-est English schools and other higher educational institutions in the state were es-tablished in such towns as Kottayam, Thiruvalla, and Alleppey—all of them in or around Kuttanad. Kottayam, a Syrian Christian stronghold, was a pioneering centre of English education in Travancore and an important centre of both the Church Mission Society and the London Mission Society. The Travancore Census of 1891 reported that among the major religious groups in the state Chris-tians had the highest proportion of "educated" in the state; they led the list with 12.59 per cent, followed by Hindus with 10.75, and Muslims with 8.18.[19]

TABLE 8: DISTRIBUTION OF LAND AMONG 108 RANDOMLY SELECTED FARMERS IN ONE VILLAGE IN KUTTANAD TALUK BY CASTE AND AMOUNT OF LAND OWNED, 1975

Area in hectares*	Nairs	Christians	Ezhavas	Others	Total
More than 12	—	6	—	—	6
6-12	1	2	—	—	3
4-6	1	—	—	—	1
2-4	2	10	—	—	12
1-2	6	28	8	—	42
4-1	12	2	4	—	18
Less than 0.4	2	16	4	4	26
Total	24	64	16	4	108

*0.4 hectares = 1 acre

The Ezhavas are also a rising caste that has gained from the economic, social, and political changes occurring in the state in general and in Kuttanad in particular. They are a low caste, immediately above the Harijans, and they have traditionally been toddy-tappers, agricultural labourers, and small cultivators, especially as subtenants. As a low caste, they were subject to various restrictions and indignities: they were forbidden to enter the temples of the higher-caste Hindus; they had to maintain a certain distance from each of the higher castes; their women had to be bare-breasted; and they suffered from many other disabilities.[20] The Ezhavas were drawn into the social and political movements that began to appear in Travancore towards the end of the nineteenth century and have been profoundly affected by them. The appearance of a great religious leader and charismatic teacher named Sri Narayana Guru gave great momentum to their movement. Drawing on the higher religious teachings of Hinduism itself, the guru attacked the caste system and urged his followers in subtle ways to disregard its rules. An often-quoted saying of the guru is: "One caste, one religion, one God for man; Man must progress whatever his religion." He soon gathered many able and devoted disciples, among whom was Kumaran Asan, who was to become one of the greatest lyric poets of Kerala in this century, a great scholar and social reformer among the Ezhavas. With a number of other concerned Ezhavas, Kumaran Asan founded in 1903 the *Sri Narayana Dharma Paripalana Yogam* (SNDPY), which became a great force in the struggle against caste discrimination and later in articulating the interests of the Ezhavas as a whole. Under the leadership of the SNDPY the Ezhavas conducted many struggles during the first half of this century. The best known among these was the Vaikkom *Satyagraha*[21] which demanded the rights of the Ezhavas and other lower castes to worship in the temples of the state and which was staged at Vaikkom, on the border of Kuttanad. In 1937 the Maharaja of Travancore made an historic proclamation which opened the doors of the temples to the low-caste Hindus of Travancore.

Although the Ezhavas of Kuttanad are still toddy-tappers, small cultivators, and agricultural labourers, the conditions of their lives have improved greatly. Toddy-tappers have one of the best organized and most effective unions in Kerala, and, Kuttanad being an important area of toddy production, the union is very strong and active in the area. They earn relatively high wages and receive other fringe benefits today. It may be interesting to note here that, since toddy-tapping is an occupation traditionally associated with the Ezhava caste and a trade secret among the members of the caste, the toddy-tappers' union is at once a labour union and a caste association. This is a pattern that is commonly found in Kuttanad as well as in the whole of Kerala. The notable exception to this pattern, of course, is agricultural labour, which acts as a great reservoir for the unemployed of all castes and occupations. Many Ezhava women work as agricultural labourers. It is not uncommon to find an Ezhava family in which the head of the household works as a toddy-tapper while the wife and two or three children are employed as agricultural labourers. With a new sense of purpose and aspirations of upward mobility that are now visible among the Ezhavas, they invest their savings in land or other profitable enterprises. A few are becoming relatively wealthy as traders, toddy shop contractors, or dealers processing and selling paddy in the black market. This relatively prosperous class of upwardly mobile Ezhavas is able to take advantage of the offers of big landlords who are anxious to dispose of excess land in the wake of new pressures for the implementation of land reforms. According to informants, the Ezhavas have been the most upwardly mobile of all castes in Kuttanad during the past two decades.

At the bottom of the caste system are the Harijans, Kuttanad's former untouchables. In 1971 Harijans formed 9.5 per cent of the population of Alleppey district and 11 per cent of the population of the 52 Kuttanad villages that lie in the district.[22] In fact, they include many castes who have their own caste occupations and who at least until recently observed caste distinctions among themselves. The most important of these are the Pulayas or Cherumars, a traditional caste of agricultural labourers. In 1961 roughly 60 per cent of all Harijans in the rural areas of the district were Pulayas.[23] Specialist castes such as the Washermen, the Blacksmiths, the Barbers, and the Coconut Tree Climbers *(Paravans)* are still largely employed in their own caste occupations, although many work as agricultural labourers on a part-time basis. According to the 1961 census, of all the Harijans in the labour force in the rural areas of the district, 67 per cent were agricultural labourers. Among the Pulayas the percentage was as high as 83.[24] The Pulayas and the other agricultural castes were agrestic slaves until the middle of the nineteenth century; after the abolition of slavery they continued to work for their former owners as attached labourers. The Harijans as a whole are landless and have been *kudikidappukars,* workers who were allowed to build their huts in the estates of the landlords for whom they worked.

The political organization and awakening of the Harijans has been among the major aspects of social change in Kuttanad during the past four decades. But unlike the Ezhavas and Nairs of Kerala who conducted their struggles for social and economic betterment through their caste associations, the Harijans have been drawn into classbased trade unions and political parties. Although in the following sections we shall be dealing directly only with the agricultural labourers, it must be borne in mind that those Harijans engaged in non-agricultural occupations also have their trade unions under the auspices of the same political party, and further that many of them are, as sympathizers or as part-time agricultural labourers, members of the agricultural labourers' union.

Some students of land and labour in India have drawn attention to the importance of understanding the cultural definitions and values attached to landownership on the one hand, and to physical labour in the fields on the other.[25] Landownership is associated with high status and has traditionally been regarded as properly belonging to the higher castes. Physical labour in the fields, on the other hand, is negatively valued and is associated with both low status and low castes.

In Kuttanad, it has been remarked, "the divorce between proprietorship of land and work in the fields was as complete as it could be."[26] Here no landowner "worth his salt" would work in the field himself or allow the members of his family to do so. It is possible that the arduous and unhygienic nature of the work required for paddy cultivation in Kuttanad may have contributed to this. In any case, one's status in society is, even today, crucially affected by one's particular relationship to the two. At one end of the scale is the landlord who does no work in the fields himself, but cultivates the land through hired labour (or in the past, tenants). At the other end are the landless labourers who work on the land for wages, but have no further attachment to the land. Among those who work in the fields the important dividing line is between those who work in their own fields only and those who sell their labour to others. Whether or not members of a family will work as wage labourers is not merely a function of its economic position; it is determined also by such factors as caste and considerations of status. An Ezhava family owning a hectare of land is much more likely to supplement its income by working in someone else's field than a Nair family in the same economic position.

Recently, Unni has drawn attention to the ways in which caste and status considerations impose serious constraints on the labour market in general and the agricultural labour market in particular. He found members of impoverished Nair families migrating to the towns to become factory workers, cooks, and waiters in restaurants. When left with no alternative except agricultural labour they preferred to migrate to a distant village where they were unknown rather than disgrace themselves in their own village.[27] Among the higher castes in Kuttanad the Syrian Christians have been traditionally less affected by these restrictions, especially as regards working in their own fields. Even among them, however, an upwardly mobile family will, at some point, stop working in the fields and start employing hired labour. This is seen as an important requirement for legitimizing its new status in the community. I came to know a Syrian Christian family which was about to arrive at this stage and which was managing to send its eldest son to college. Although the father still worked in the field, the "college boy" not only stopped participating in such work but also felt ashamed whenever his rough and blistered hands became visible to his college and hostel mates. In fact, he was attempting by various means to make his hands softer like those of his college friends from higher-class families.

The negative value attached to work is much greater in the case of women. Among the higher castes it is rare for women to work in the fields and even rarer for them to work in others' fields as wage labourers. Unni has observed that in Palghat impoverished Nair women heads of households would engage in clandestine prostitution rather than work as agricultural labourers. Yet, in Kuttanad roughly 46 per cent of all agricultural labourers are estimated to be women. It is clear that they are drawn predominantly from the Ezhavas and Harijans—even more so than is the case with men labourers. A Syrian Christian family of small landholders may make use of the labour of its female members for its own fields, but if it must supplement the family income with outside work it would be the men who would go out to work. In the past, Nair and Syrian Christian women rarely participated in any kind of wage labour; today many among them from the poorer families can be seen participating in harvesting, which is considered lucrative in Kuttanad, although they still will not participate in other types of agricultural work.

PATTERN OF LANDOWNERSHIP

It is clear from our foregoing analysis that while the congruence between caste and landownership is still quite visible, it is a fluid one and it has been changing greatly over the past hundred years. Obviously, some castes have benefitted from these processes of change and replaced others as landowners. But caste can no longer give us an accurate description of the structure of land tenure in Kuttanad. The relative dissociation between caste and landownership has meant that the ownership and control over land have become even more crucial in determining one's position and life chances in society than in the past. Ironically, the possibility of owning land has presented itself to the low-caste man just at the time Kuttanad has become known as one of the areas with the lowest per capita availability of land in the country. There is little doubt, however, that what land is available is very unequally distributed. Unfortunately, the researcher who attempts to collect information on landownership in Kuttanad at the present time faces a serious problem; those who own above the legal limit of six hectares or even close to it are reluctant, if not altogether unwilling, to provide him with the relevant information. Typically, a landlord discloses only those lands he owns on paper as his own, the rest, the excess land, having been transferred to other names already. Hence, recent studies on the pattern of landownership in Kuttanad are very likely to underestimate the extent of landlordism there.

The Kuttanad Development Project gives extensive recent data on the pattern of landholdings in the region. These are reproduced in Tables 9 and 10. These figures indicate that in 1973 36 per cent of the cultivators of Kuttanad owned less than 0.4 hectares of land accounting for only 12 per cent of the area; 86 per cent of all cultivators owning less than 2 hectares each accounted for only 60 per cent of the area, the remaining 14 per cent accounting for 40 per cent of the area. If the agricultural labourers who form roughly 70 per cent of the total labour force in agriculture are taken into account (see Table 4 in Chapter 2), the result is the percentage distribution as given in Table 11. It shows the top 1 per cent of the population engaged in agriculture as owning nearly 20 per cent of the land. In Kerala 2 hectares is generally taken to be the dividing line between small and big farmers. By this standard, 5 per cent of the population are big farmers accounting for 40 per cent of the land. What is most striking, however, is the fact that 80 per cent of the entire labour force in agriculture is landless or near landless, owning less than 0.4 hectares.

TABLE 9: PATTERN OF LANDHOLDINGS IN KUTTANAD, JUNE 1973

Holdings in Hectares*	Alleppey District		Kottayam District		Total	
	No. of Culti-vators	Extent of Holdings (ha)	No. of Culti-vators	Extent of Holdings (ha)	No. of Cultiv-vators	Extent of Holdings (ha)
less than 0.4	10,112	4,166	6,464	2,556	16,576	6,722
0.4-1	7,723	6,667	4,460	3,981	12,183	10,648
1-2	6,203	9,841	4,957	7,182	11,160	17,023
2-4	3,816	8,696	1,215	3,503	5,031	12,199
4-6	1,013	4,312	238	1,072	1,251	5,384
more than 6	201	4,333	141	1,323	342	5,656
Total	29,068	38,015	17,475	19,617	46,543	57,632

*0.4 hectares = 1 acre
Source: Government of Kerala, *Report on Kuttanad Development Project,* 1974, p. 17

TABLE 10: PATTERN OF LANDHOLDINGS IN KUTTANAD, JUNE 1973—PERCENTAGES

Holdings in Hectares*	Alleppey District		Kottayam District		Total	
	No. of Culti-vators	Extent of Holdings (ha)	No. of Culti-vators	Extent of Holdings (ha)	No. of Culti-vators	Extent of Holdings (ha)
less than 0.4	35	11	37	13	36	12
0.4-1	27	18	26	20	26	18
1-2	21	26	28	37	24	30
2-4	13	23	7	18	11	21
4-6	3	11	1	5	3	9
more than 6	0.7	11	0.8	7	0.7	10
Total	100	100	100	100	100	100

*0.4 hectares = 1 acre
Source: Government of Kerala, *Report on Kuttanad Development Project,* 1974, p. 17

The 1961 census gives some information about landholding for the rural areas

TABLE 11: PERCENTAGE DISTRIBUTION OF THE LABOUR FORCE IN AGRICULTURE IN RELATION TO LANDHOLDINGS

Extent of Holdings (ha)	Percentage of the Labour Force in Agriculture	Percentage of Area Owned
landless and less than 0.4	80	11.7
0.4-2	15	48.0
2-4	3	21.2
4-6	1.8	9.3
more than 6	0.2	9.8
Total	100	100

Source: Compiled from Tables 2 and 9.

of Alleppey district as a whole (see Table 12). These figures show that only 5.3 per cent of the cultivators are big farmers owning 2 or more hectares of land. However, roughly 1 per cent of the cultivators hold 6 or more hectares of land. It is significant that Kuttanad taluk, which has the largest *kayal padasekharams* (paddy fields in the lake area), also stands out as having the highest proportion of large landowners. In the taluk, 35.7 per cent of all cultivators have holdings of 2 or more hectares, 13 per cent hold 6 or more hectares, and 1.7 per cent are very large landowners with holdings of 20 hectares or more. Thus, out of the 27 in Alleppey district who own 20 or more hectares of land, 20 are in this taluk. The fact that these figures represent a sample of 20 per cent means that this taluk may have a total of 100 landowners of this kind. This need not be an overestimation. It has been well known that there is a small class of large cultivators concentrated in the kayal areas of lower Kuttanad. A sample survey conducted in the kayal areas of Kuttanad by two economists from Kerala University during the crop year of 1962 reveals a pattern of large landholdings that stands out, as the authors themselves remark, in sharp contrast to the subsistence farms in the rest of Kerala. Their findings are given in Table 13. The average area of the holdings here exceeded 60 hectares. As the authors remark, "while 90 per cent of the holdings in Kerala are below 2.5 acres, an equal proportion of holdings in the *kayal* area are above 25 acres."[28]

It is true that there have been some changes in the situation since the early 1960's when these two sets of data were collected. It is necessary to examine in particular whether and to what extent recent land reform measures have affected the land tenure system of Kuttanad.

Kerala has passed more extensive and more radical land reform legislation than most other states in India. In general, these land reform measures had three

TABLE 12: DISTRIBUTION OF SAMPLE HOUSEHOLDS ENGAGED IN CULTIVATION BY
SIZE OF LAND CULTIVATED FOR RURAL AREAS OF THE DISTRICT AND TALUKS

Extent of land (hectares)*	Alleppey District	Shertalai	Ambalapuzha	Kuttanad	Thiruvalla	Chengannur	Kartigapally	Mavelikara
less than 0.4	14,203	1,003	296	273	3,832	3,105	1,245	4,449
0.4-1.9	7,599	630	195	485	2,148	1,495	588	2,057
2.0-3.9	771	44	41	174	138	94	97	183
4.0-5.9	224	10	7	95	26	25	21	40
6.0-11.9	158	5	3	99	15	9	10	17
12.0-19.9	41	—	—	34	2	3	2	—
more than 20.0	27	1	1	20	—	—	3	2
Unspecified	4	0	0	0	1	2	0	1
No. of Cultivating Households	23,027	1,693	543	1,181	6,162	6,733	1,966	6,749

*0.4 hectares = 1 acre

Source: *District Census Handbook, Alleppey,* 1961, p. 131.

TABLE 13: DISTRIBUTION OF SELECTED HOLDINGS IN THE KAYAL AREA
OF KUTTANAD BY SIZE

Area in hectares*	Holdings	
	Number	Percentage
0.0-4.0	2	5
4.4-10.0	2	5
10.4-16.0	6	15
16.4-24.0	8	20
24.4-40.0	12	30
40.4-100.0	6	15
100.4-200.0	3	7.5
200.4 and above	1	2.5
All	40	100

*0.4 hectares = 1 acre
Source: V. R. Pillai and P. G. K. Panikar, *Land Reclamation in Kerala* (New
York: Asia Publishing House, 1965), p. 48.

immediate goals: a) to confer ownership rights on the tenant cultivators and to
abolish all intermediaries; b) to protect the kudikidappukars by conferring upon
them permanent occupancy and even ownership rights; and c) to attain a more
equal distribution of the land by putting a ceiling on holdings and distributing the
surplus land to the landless. The first two goals seem to have been largely
achieved in Kuttanad. The third, which, if achieved, would have radical implica-
tion for the pattern of landholdings in Kuttanad, still remains an unattained and
distant one.[29]

The first comprehensive and radical land reform legislation in the state was
the "Kerala Agrarian Relations Act" passed by its first Communist government
(also the first government of the new state) in 1960. This and other radical measures initiated by the government led to the eruption in the state of what is generally described by the opponents of the government as a "liberation struggle" led
mainly by the Syrian Christian churches and the Nair Service Society (NSS). The
government was dismissed shortly thereafter by the president of India for its failure to maintain "law and order." Meanwhile, the Agrarian Relations Act had
been declared unconstitutional by the Supreme Court of the country. The Congress government that followed enacted a fresh act which, while retaining most
of the provisions of the previous act generally softened the latter's radical provisions. A long series of legislation and amendments has been passed since then by
governments with differing or even opposing political philosophies, each one
often modifying or even repealing the previous ones. The latest in the series
were enacted by the United Front government led by the Communist

Party of India but supported also by the Congress Party.[30] The "Kerala Land Reforms (Amendment) Act 1971" similar in many respects but with much less radical and far-reaching provisions, came into effect retroactively on 1 January 1970.

The results of all these have been, at best, modest. The greatest achievement so far has been in conferring fixity of tenure and full ownership rights to the tenant cultivators and to the kudikidappukars. The only measure that has benefitted the bottom section of the population has been the latter one. (It has already been observed that tenants in Kuttanad include its wealthiest and largest landowners.) Today it is difficult to find a *kudikidappukaran* who does not own his own homestead. Even in the occasional case of a dispute that has resulted in a lawsuit in the court, the kudikidappukaran occupies and takes the yields of the land pending the court's decision. All have not received the same amount, however. The amount ranged from 2 to 10 cents.[31] Of the 75 in our survey who received *kudikidappu* land, 43 received 10 cents each, 25 between 5 and 10 cents, and 7 below 5 cents. It is not clear why some got less, although it seems likely that the plots housing their huts amounted to only that much. In any case, there is some evidence that without the organized strength and the militancy of the kudikidappukars even these results would not have been achieved so fast. As soon as the act came into effect, the *Karshaka Thozhilali* union organized the hutment dwellers to "grab" their land before the landowners might outmanoeuvre them and deny them their right to the land by some pretext or other. They began establishing their ownership rights to the lands by putting up fences around them and plucking coconuts and other crops. Although this movement led to a certain amount of violence, most landowners in Kuttanad saw the futility of a physical confrontation with the organized strength of the union and came forward to settle the transfer of the small patches of land amicably. That the "due process of the law" would have resulted in the kudikidappukars receiving much less is borne out by the experience of other areas. According to a recent study by K. C. Alexander,[32] out of the estimated 400,000 kudikidappukars in the state, only 350,000 had applied to the land boards for ownership rights, and of these only 109,000 had been successful. It is significant that 101,000 applications were rejected. In one midland village in Kottayam district the achievements of the kudikidappukars have been much less impressive than in Kuttanad. There it was the general practice of the landowners to allot to their kudikidappukars less than the 10 cents prescribed, and what is worse, to evict them from their homesteads and to shift them to a barren and unproductive piece of land in some corner of their property.

It is, however, with regard to the measures to put upper ceilings on holdings that the legislation has been most seriously infringed. Although the Agrarian Relations Act of 1960 never came into effect, it created panic in the hearts of the landowners. Despite the fact that the legislation of 1963 exempted Kuttanad from the ceiling on holdings, they knew it was a matter of time before their land, too, would come under these provisions, and their sense of insecurity only grew

worse. They began to dispose of some of their lands and to diversify their investments into plantations (exempted from the ceiling even to this day) and business
in and out of Kerala. It is interesting to note that most of the rich landowning
families of Kuttanad today have such investments, some in Tamil Nadu, and a
small number have even left Kuttanad altogether. In any event, all the landlords
in Kuttanad (with a very few notable exceptions) quickly made sure that they had
no excess land (that is, land exceeding the ceiling prescribed in the act) on paper
by registering all potential excess land in the names of relatives, friends, labourers (in some cases without their knowledge), and even non-existent people.
Significantly, the officials of the labour union and other CPI(M) workers have
bitterly complained that under the present government's land legislation all
transfers effected between 1958 and 1963 were deemed valid. But even after that
date the landowners have been able to devise various ingenious means to circum-
vent the law and to sell or transfer land. In one case, a landowner had one of his
wife's relatives file a lawsuit in the court claiming tenancy rights in his land and
supporting his claim with false documents. As the legal process took its course,
the landlord agreed to "settle" the dispute amicably, thus transferring excess
land into his relative's name.

According to information obtained from the Collector's Office in Alleppey,
the excess land (as declared by the landlords) in Alleppey district is only
1,614.55 hectares, which represents only a fraction of the actual excess land in
the area. Out of this, the land board, established by the government, has autho-
rized the takeover of 1,329.1 hectares. So far, 1,162.59 hectares have actually
been taken possession of. It is significant to note that 731 hectares of this land
was taken from the famed "kayal king," Murickan, which constituted a special
case since these lands were not taken over under provisions of the land reforms
act. Although plans for redistribution abounded, no land had actually been redistributed in Kuttanad up to September 1975.

In sum, it may be said that land ceiling measures have had little effect on the
pattern of landholding in Kuttanad.[33] In 1975 in a single village in Kuttanad
taluk, 12 landowners cultivated more than 28 hectares of land, of whom 7 held
more than 40 hectares each. Many of them also had plantations and other property outside Kuttanad. While this pattern is not typical of the region as a whole, it
was not very different from what obtained in the neighbouring villages of the
kayal areas of Kuttanad taluk. It is remarkable that this pattern does not differ
greatly from that of the early 1960's (Tables 12 and 13). However, it must be
added that some redistribution of land is certainly occurring in Kuttanad through
processes other than land reform measures *per se*. In the prevailing conditions of
uncertainty and insecurity many landlords continue to dispose of their excess
land, although they must now do it illegally. There is an emerging prosperous
class, drawn from landless labourers and small peasants, that buys this land.
Although an interesting phenomenon, accurate information regarding this class
and its behaviour is not available. It seems certain, however, that these upwardly

mobile men have not been dependent solely on agricultural labour for their earnings; rather, they have been lucky to have had alternative or additional sources of income such as toddy-tapping and processing paddy for sale in the black market. Furthermore, they seem to be drawn predominantly from the Ezhava community which, in general, has much greater access to such sources of income than the Pulayas.

CLASS AND CLASS CONFLICT

So far, in attempting to describe Kuttanad's social structure, its castes, its pattern of landholdings, and the extent to which different sections of its agricultural population participate in labour have been dealt with. Although some of the important cleavages in Kuttanad society have been described, this discussion has not amounted to a description of its class structure. This is indeed a difficult task. The categories developed by Lenin, Mao, and other Marxist analysts are not entirely suitable for Kuttanad, and their mechanical application is likely to mislead and confuse rather than enhance an understanding. To see why this is so, three important features of Kuttanad's agrarian class structure must be considered. First, in Kuttanad it is not easy, and perhaps much less useful, to distinguish the capitalist landlord from the feudal landlord or even from the rich peasant as theoreticians of the CPI(M) do. This is not only because tenants and sharecroppers have virtually disappeared from Kuttanad after the recent land reforms. Even before that the so-called tenants in Kuttanad included many capitalist farmers with substantial holdings who leased out more land for cultivation on a commercial basis. Second, independent small-holders who perform all or most of their work with family labour and who do not hire themselves out as wage labourers—the well-known middle peasants—are practically non-existent or fast disappearing.[34] In Kuttanad, relatively small peasants cultivating less than a hectare of land employ some wage labour; even the smallest owners who hire themselves out for part of the year have to hire labour at harvest time. Third, Kuttanad has an unusually large rural proletariat of landless or near-landless wage labourers.

The problem centres on the question of the mode of production in agriculture and specifically on the dual-economy thesis. Without entering into the long debate that Indian Marxists have carried on during the past several years, it is neither possible nor fruitful to distinguish different ''sectors'' of the economy in Kuttanad.[35] If anything, several important features of Kuttanad's agriculture— its relatively large-scale and profit-oriented commercial farming, its large class of wage labourers, and the dissolution of most pre-capitalist forms of relationships between landowners and labourers—point to a relatively high degree of capitalist development (or perhaps more accurately, underdevelopment). But even the conception of capitalist farming is not likely to prove satisfactory if Kuttanad's agriculture is not considered within the wider context of an underdeveloped and neo-colonial economic and social system, itself part of a worldwide imperialist capitalism. Such an economy and society has its own features which need to be examined in detail.[36]

The concern of this study has been predominantly with the most profound cleavage that has emerged in Kuttanad, that between the rural proletariat and the employers of their labour, a group of people who may be loosely described as the farmers. This cleavage is objective because it is rooted in antagonistic productive relations. It is also subjective because both the categories have emerged as organized, acting, struggling, and self-conscious classes who stand in opposition to each other. In the context of politics and class struggle in Kuttanad these appear to be the most relevant categories.

The making of the agricultural labour class, the class of the rural proletariat—its rise, organization, and growth to self-consciousness, will be discussed in some detail in the next chapter. The farmers see themselves as a group only in so far as they stand in opposition to the agricultural labourers whose organized interests and demands are perceived as being counter to their own. Their own organization and articulation of interests will be discussed only in the context of the struggles of the agricultural labourers. However, before closing this chapter it is useful to make a few remarks that may help to clarify the nature of this amorphous category.

The analysis provided in this chapter makes it clear that the farmers are a heterogeneous group differentiated by caste, landed wealth, and power. They range from small peasants to big landlords, cultivating anywhere from a fraction of a hectare to over fifty hectares. If we accept the data on landholdings provided by the Kuttanad Development Project as given in Tables 9 and 10, we see that only 15 per cent of the farmers of Kuttanad own more than 2 hectares of land, 50 per cent between 0.4 and 2 hectares, and 35 per cent less than 0.4 hectares. A little less than 1 per cent of the farmers are estimated to own more than 6 hectares, the legal limit in Kerala at present. They are clearly a privileged minority. Among them are the tiny class of the rural rich whose presence in Kuttanad is very conspicuous indeed. A casual traveller in Kuttanad's waterways is sure to see the many expensive and beautiful motor launches with the names of Kuttanad's important families written on them in bold letters. Their large houses with their Western-style living and dining rooms, refrigerators, electric appliances, and in some cases even running water made available with their own private pumps, stand out in sharp contrast to the tiny thatched huts of the kudikidappukars. The largest number of farmers are, of course, those cultivating between 0.4 and 2 hectares of land. In Kuttanad, a person cultivating 2 hectares of paddy fields is considered relatively well-off. Even one cultivating between 1 and 2 hectares is *petit bourgeois*. Farmers holding less than this amount, especially those with less than 0.4 hectares (36 per cent), must live a precarious life if they do not have alternate sources of income. Although precise information about their occupational patterns is not available, it seems certain that many of them have other occupations, such as toddy-tapping or part-time agricultural labour. This is especially true about those cultivating less than 0.4 hectares of land. It is possible that a substantial number of them work also as agricultural labourers. In Kerala anyone who owns some land feels entitled to be classified as a cultivator rather than an agricultural labourer.

Despite their heterogeneity, the farmers of Kuttanad perceive common interests *vis-à-vis* the agricultural labourers. Although even very small farmers hire labour during some part of the year, it is clear that wage labour is much less crucial to them than to the larger farmers whose position is at present absolutely dependent on the employment of wage labour. Many of the larger farmers have attempted to reduce this dependence by mechanizing the farming operations, but as we shall see later, this attempt met with violent opposition from the labour unions. Nevertheless, the small farmers are no less hostile to the demands of the agricultural labourers' union and complain that they are unable to pay the high wages. Their resentment is greater if they belong to the higher castes.[37] The smaller farmers who also work as wage labourers are in a different position, however. They are at least potential allies of the agricultural labourers. Some are members of the agricultural labour union; many lend their support to the agricultural labourers' cause.

4

The Agricultural Labourers

In this chapter the evolution and growth of the agricultural labour force of Kuttanad, its position in the social structure, its relative economic status, and changes in the conditions of its members' life and work will be discussed.

EVOLUTION AND GROWTH

In India, government departments and agencies have not always followed a consistent definition in referring to agricultural labourers. This is a serious handicap in attempting to study the size and growth of the agricultural labour force; at best, such discrepancies can be pointed out when they occur. For purposes of this study the operational definition of agricultural labourers used by the First Agricultural Labour Inquiry conducted under the auspices of the Indian government will be adopted. It defined an agricultural labour family as one in which either the head of the family or 50 per cent or more of its earners reported agricultural labour as their major occupation.[1] It is clear that agricultural labourers also engage in other occupations. Some own patches of land which they cultivate. Therefore, it is not possible to draw a sharp line between an agricultural labourer and a very small or poor peasant. However, because of the negative value attached to the occupation of the agricultural labourer all over India, many, especially among the impoverished higher castes, tend to define themselves as cultivators if there is any possibility of doing so. Hence, it can be presumed that the census returns would underestimate rather than overestimate the number of agricultural labourers.

Who are the agricultural labourers of today? When did this class begin to appear in Kuttanad? Accurate information about these questions does not exist, and it is therefore very difficult to provide any adequate answers. There is a long-standing and widely held view which is by now fairly well documented that the integration of India's village economy into the British colonial economy thwarted the industrialization of the country and created an agrarian crisis.[2] Some writers who hold this view have, however, tended to idealize the precapitalist village community in India as self-sufficient and even socialistic and have argued that the present class of agricultural labourers emerged during British rule and was a product of the agrarian crisis created by imperialism.[3] While there is little doubt that the proportion of landless labourers has been steadily increasing during the last two hundred years, there is now ample evidence that in South India at least, a class of landless agricultural labourers has existed for a long time and that this class was mostly in servitude. The most important study in this respect, that of Dharma Kumar, is confined to the old Madras Presidency which includes Malabar, but not the princely states of Travancore and Cochin.[4] Other sources, however, confirm that the situation in the two princely states was not very different from that of Malabar.[5] Significantly, Dharma Kumar notes that in the old Madras presidency Malabar district was the most notorious of all for the rigours of its slavery and the wretchedness of the slaves. Almost every British administrator who went there in the early nineteenth century was prompted to remark on it. Moreover, unfree labourers were frequently concentrated on the wet lands or the irrigated rice areas, particularly in the west coast districts. Agrestic servitude seems to have been of particular importance in the first half of the nineteenth century for rice cultivation and for agricultural work in general. During this period the bulk of the agricultural labour force was in servitude and belonged to the agricultural labour castes. Almost every member of the slave castes was an agricultural labourer. That is, 10 to 15 per cent of the total population were agricultural labourers. It would appear, therefore, that agrestic servitude must have been an important factor in paddy cultivation in Kuttanad before the abolition of slavery.

An important feature of agrestic slavery in Kerala, as also elsewhere in south India, was the close connection of the forms of servitude with the caste system. Most types of servile status were hereditary, and most slaves belonged to the lowest castes, particularly *Cherumars* or Pulayas. It is instructive that Buchanan used the term *Cheruman* as synonymous with the word *adima,* or slave.

The main forms of agrestic servitude were slavery and serfdom. The slaves were bought and sold; the serfs were born into a state in which they owed service to their masters. It is interesting that three important tenancies of land were also applicable to slaves. These were:

1) *jenmom,* which meant full ownership or birthright;
2) *kanom,* a long-term lease which entitled the proprietor to receive periodically renewable fees;

3) *pattom,* or regular lease, whereby the slave was hired out for an annual sum.

The slave trade was banned in Travancore in 1812, and slavery was completely abolished in 1855. However, it seems that less formal and probably less rigorous forms of servitude continued to flourish until recently. Capitalist development and the new factories and plantations opened up at least some new opportunities for agricultural labour. It must be pointed out, however, that these new opportunities were available to the untouchable castes only to a limited extent. The plantations in the hill regions which would have absorbed labour from the very bottom of society recruited Tamil labour in large numbers. This limited the opportunities for Travancore workers, especially for those from the distant coastal areas such as Kuttanad. In the factories recruitment was limited by conditions imposed by the caste system. The untouchable workers would be the last to be considered, and then only for positions at the very bottom.[6] Nevertheless, the coir industry was a labour-intensive one and also created outside jobs, where the raw material was processed and made ready for the factories. Therefore, at least a portion of the Harijans were able to take advantage of the new opportunities in the coir industry.

No exact information exists about the changes in the proportion of agricultural labourers in Travancore or in the country as a whole. They were estimated to number 7.5 million in 1882 and 21 million or one-fifth of those engaged in agriculture in 1921. By 1931 their number had risen to 33 million or roughly 33 per cent of those engaged in agriculture and in 1951 to 35 million or 37.5 per cent of agriculturists.[7] Exact changes in the proportion of landless labourers since 1951 are difficult to obtain because of the changes in the mode of census classification. In many areas of the country they are known to have increased greatly. In 1911 53.2 per cent of the population of Travancore were engaged in agriculture. Agricultural labour made up 6.7 per cent of this. By 1951 the agricultural population had increased to 57.2 per cent. And 19.2 per cent of these were agricultural labourers. However, this remarkable increase seems to have been at least in part an artifact of the differences in census enumeration between 1911 and 1951. Many who were treated as agricultural workers in 1951 would have been classified as domestic servants in 1911 when they were expected to perform many household duties besides farm labour.[8] Nevertheless, it seems safe to conclude that the increase in the proportion of agricultural workers in Travancore has been quite substantial.

Recent census figures for Alleppey district, which are more reliable, show a trend of increase that is even more striking. Changes in the population of Alleppey district between 1961 and 1971 are shown in Table 14. It is important to note that as the proportion of the work force in agriculture increased during this decade from 37 per cent to 46.7 per cent, the number of cultivators fell from 109,566 to 95,798. The number of agricultural labourers increased by 57 per

TABLE 14: DISTRIBUTION OF THE WORK FORCE ENGAGED IN AGRICULTURE IN ALLEPPEY DISTRICT, 1961 AND 1971

Total Work Force	Work Force in Agriculture	Cultivators	Agricultural Labourers	Work Force in Agriculture as Percentage of Total Workers	Agricultural Labourers as Percentage of the Work Force in Agriculture	Agricultural Labourers as Percentage of Total Workers
1961 610,424	226,400	109,566	116,834	37	51.6	19
1971 598,468	279,279	95,798	183,481	46.7	65.7	31

Source: *District Census Handbook, Alleppey,* 1961 and 1971.

cent during this period.[9] The increase was considerable both in absolute and relative terms. It seems certain, therefore, that Alleppey district and Kuttanad are among the areas that have seen a tremendous growth in the size and proportion of the agricultural labour force. It seems probable that this is related not only to the deindustrialization of the area but also to the proletarianization of some tenants and small cultivators.

POSITION IN THE SOCIAL STRUCTURE

In discussing the position of Kuttanad's agricultural labourers, two points must be kept in mind. First, the changes that have been occurring in their position over the years makes this a very difficult task; therefore, when not otherwise noted, the conditions we described will be those that obtained in the 1930's. It was by the end of that decade that the changes became much more rapid and far-reaching. Second, agricultural labourers belong predominantly to the "scheduled" and "backward" castes with the result that the conditions of their life and work have also been governed by caste rules and practices. Their rights and duties and their relationship with their employers were not limited to work and wages alone, but penetrated every aspect of their lives. Hence, in describing their position in the social structure, and particularly their relationship to their employers, no attempt will be made to distinguish or separate class relations from caste relations. True, the numbers of agricultural labourers gradually swelled as impoverished members of the higher castes began joining them. Nevertheless, the Harijans and the other lower castes still make up the vast majority. The conditions described will apply predominantly to the Harijans.[10]

Traditionally, there were three kinds of agricultural labourers in Kuttanad: *paniyal,* or attached labourer; *panathal* (also known as *onappanikkaran*), or semi-attached labourer; and *purathal* (literally, ''outsider''), or completely free casual labourer. The bulk of the labour force was made up of attached labourers. The labourer, together with his entire family, was attached to a landlord and was generally known by the latter's name as *Murickan's pulayan, Mamkompan's pulayan,* and so on. The adult men of his household performed the heavier work such as bunding and ploughing; the women and children attended to such operations as weeding, transplanting, and harvesting. Even the smaller children had their duties to perform. They would run errands or chase the crows and other birds from the fields. It seems that when the Harijan children began to attend schools in large numbers in the 1940's and 1950's they faced the open displeasure of the landlords.

The labourer's attachment to the landlord was further strengthened by the fact that he was also a kudikidappukaran permitted to put up his residence in a portion of his landlord's property.[11] He usually built his hut in a convenient location from where he could watch over the crops. Around his hut he was often allowed to cultivate a few odd crops—bananas, tapioca, and vegetables—for his own use. Apart from this he was not entitled to any produce from the land.[12] This rule was very strictly enforced in regard to such valuable produce as coconuts. During festivals such as *Onam* (Kerala's harvest festival and New Year season) he made gifts of bananas and other vegetables to the landlord and received presents of mostly clothing in return.

Being doubly bound to the landlord as attached labourer and kudikidappu-karan, the labourer was expected to be at the disposal of his master almost twenty-four hours a day. As noted before, the conditions of punja cultivation require constant vigilance, especially during the monsoons. Floods may threaten or even breach a weak bund and thus endanger an entire crop. It was the labourer's duty to be alert and prepared for emergency operations on such occasions. Most landlord families had head-labourers to supervise agricultural operations, and they had special responsibilities in this regard. In the romanticized version of the bygone system that is often heard in Kuttanad and is sometimes found even in books, one hears of such instances as that of a labourer "keeping incessant watch over the vulnerable bunds, throwing himself across the breach which yawned before him to stem the tide of the rushing water."[13]

Furthermore, the labourer and members of his family were required to perform odd jobs of all kinds for the landlord and his household. These ranged from cutting firewood to beating up his landlord's enemies. Every prominent landlord family maintained a group of Pulaya *Thugs*. Some informants report that it was not uncommon for two groups of Pulayas to engage in physical fights for the sake of two rival landlords to whom they belonged. The extent and nature of these duties were restricted by the rules of untouchability. Thus no Pulaya performed such household duties as cooking for Brahmins, Nairs, or other upper castes. A limited variety of household tasks such as grinding grain was performed for the Syrian Christians, who seemed to have been less affected by the caste rules of purity and pollution. There were no required payments for these services, although the labourer was likely to receive some free gifts from time to time. It must be pointed out that the very privilege of being a kudikidappukaran was considered to be a favour from the landlord who expected various services in return. It is instructive that even today when a person wants to assert his independence against someone or to free himself from some unreasonable demands, he is wont to say, "Do you think I am your kudikidappukaran?"

Despite the fact that the labourer was the cultivator of the land in a genuine sense, he had no rights in the land. A kudikidappukaran could be evicted at any time, although an act of this kind without sufficient justification was liable to affect the landlord's good name in the community. Most people can remember instances of a landlord appearing with his thugs one fine morning to evict a kudi-kidappukaran who seriously angered him for some reason. Within minutes, the labourer's few belongings would be thrown out of the hut, his hut pulled down or even burned to ashes, and the recalcitrant worker thrown out on the road. Very rarely, however, did a landlord's cruelty reach such proportions; more often the kudikidappukaran would be given sufficient notice so that he had time to approach another landlord for space to build a hut. Since there was a shortage of labour in the past it was not difficult to find another landlord willing to give refuge to a kudikidappukaran. In the very rare case of one who failed to find any kudikidappu land there was the last resort of occupying some *puramboke* or government land. It is interesting to note that evictions of kudikidappukars continued to be practised in Kuttanad as late as the 1940's and even the early 1950's, and it was a common punishment given to the agricultural labourers who became active in the labour movement in its initial years. The fact that this practice came to an end in Kuttanad before it did so in other parts of the state is in no small part owing to the organized strength of the agricultural labour union.

Despite the early development of capitalism in Kuttanad, the relationship between farmers and labourers remained pre-capitalist and authoritarian, at least until the early 1940's. There were aspects of this relationship that smacked of slavery and may have been survivals of the past. In any case, the labourer addressed the farmer as "master" *(thampuran* or *thampran)* or lord *(melan),* and referred to himself as slave *(adiyan)* in the presence of the former. It is interesting to note that the Christian labourers often used various kinship terms such as *appachan* (father) or *achayan* (elder brother) to address their Christian landlords.

Undoubtedly, caste and caste prejudice have been important factors in this relationship. Nowhere else did caste restrictions assume such systematization and rigidity as they did in Kerala. Here the Pulaya labourer was not only an untouchable but also an unseeable, and he was required to keep off the public roads at the approach of a higher caste person.[14] Of course, the severity of these practices had been blunted by the various forces of social change mentioned in the last chapter. Moreover, in Kuttanad the labourers dealt mostly with Nairs and Syrian Christians who practised milder forms of caste restrictions than the Namboothiri Brahmins. Nevertheless, caste, caste prejudice, and stereotyping were of considerable importance in the 1930's. Even today, few among the upper castes believe that the Harijans are their equals in native intelligence or moral qualities. I found many upper caste men, including many Syrian Christians, who attributed the inferior social status of the labourers to their presumed inferior stock.[15]

Not very long ago, the untouchable labourer of Travancore was denied the use of public highways, conveyances, common wells, and hospitals. He had no access to bazaars and was not allowed to build tiled houses or wear valuable ornaments. As mentioned earlier, his womenfolk could not wear upper garments and had to appear bare-breasted.[16] By the 1930's these restrictions had, by and large, ceased to apply.[17] However, even at that time the labourer was not expected to educate his children or to give them names in use among the upper castes. He used linguistic forms notably different from those used by the upper castes. Generally speaking, he used abject or diminutive words to refer to himself, members of his family and to his possessions. Thus his children were "calves" *(kidangal)*, his paddy "chaff" *(pathiru)*, his rice "gruel" *(kadi)*, his house "hut" *(madam)*, and his money "coppers" *(chempukashu)*. Furthermore, there were many rules, explicit and implicit, that governed the behaviour of the labourer in the presence of his master (and members of his master's class in general). They ensured that in his movements, in his posture, in his demeanor, in his choice of words, in his dress, in word and deed, he showed deference, humility, and submissiveness. As for payment of wages for his work, the labourer was expected to receive it with both hands at the time the master chose to give it, without complaint. Any attempt to dispute the master's figures or to bargain was considered a sign of arrogance. And, in general, few signs of arrogance went unpunished. Even in the 1930's and 1940's, says S. K. Das, one of the first two organizers of agricultural labourers in Kuttanad, a labourer who dared to wear a moustache, to crop his hair fashionably, to appear well dressed, or worst of all, not to take off his head-dress in the presence of an upper-caste person, was likely to receive a good beating.

Stories abound which recount the exploitation of Harijan women by landlords, most notably Syrian Christian, the major land-owning caste in Kuttanad. Typically, a landlord would have one of his young Pulayas called away from his hut to have some odd job performed in the fields or elsewhere, and he would then appear in the Pulaya's hut to exploit some young woman in his household. In any case, such stories are part of the folklore in Kuttanad which neither the Syrian Christian landlords nor the Pulaya labourers deny. In fact, some Syrian Christians even seemed chauvinistic about it, claiming that the young Pulaya leaders, fair-skinned and smart, had Syrian Christian blood flowing in their veins. "Do you think," they asked, "that they could have come out of the *Pulaya* stock?" From the Pulayas' side, an old man gave a rather strange and amusing explanation of the sickle that appears on the flag of the Communist Party. According to him its origin goes back to the time when the young Pulaya ladies, disgusted and fed up with the unending sexual advances of their thampuran, finally raised their sickles against him in the field. Many local people, including the circle inspector (the police officer of the area) considered the landlords thoroughly immoral in this respect. Whatever the truth of these assertions, it is clear that since the 1940's and early 1950's the social climate has changed quite drastically, and few landlords have dared to indulge in this pastime.

The relationship between the landlord and his attached labourer has been characterized as a system of patron-client relationships.[18] Strong personal bonds and personal loyalty seem to have existed between many Pulayas and their masters. Mention has already been made of the idealized version of this relationship in which the loyal Pulaya is said to have been willing to risk his life to protect his master and his master's property. When a human sacrifice was deemed necessary, it is said, during the construction of a bund, there was not wanting a loyal Pulaya volunteering for the "honour." The following story is typical of many which describe the loyalty of the Pulayas in the old days. It was narrated by the municipal chairman of Alleppey who comes from the famous Chalayil family, which is said to have pioneered kayal cultivation in Kuttanad. One of his great ancestors had been building a bund and had planned to have a Pulaya worker sacrificed. It had been arranged in advance that as the bund was nearing completion a selected Pulaya worker would be left to remain in the water. The other workers were then to cover him up quickly with the mud and garbage, burying him alive inside the bund. As the pile of mud and garbage rose up to the Pulaya's neck, so the story goes, he raised his voice and said calmly to his master, "My tampran, why did you not tell me early? Would I not have voluntarily sacrificed myself for your sake?" Whatever the truth of these stories, a very high value seems to have always been attached to loyalty in this sytem. From the landlord the labourer could expect to receive various gifts, especially on such occasions in his family as death and marriage. His greatest benefit seems to have been the sense of security that the system gave him. As long as the relationship remained without strain he could count on his master for protection and care in the event of accident or illness. Needless to say, it was in his interest to do his utmost to keep the relationship without strain.

Many people in Kuttanad, especially farmers and government officials, speak of the old arrangements in glowing terms. The labourers, they say, were happy and contented and would have remained so even today if it were not for the communist politicians who have been arousing and misleading them. An old Nair politician said that the Pulayas had only two needs: to have a roof over their heads and to have their bellies filled. As long as these two needs were satisfied, they were happy and contented. If only the farmers had been a little more humane and conscientious about looking after these needs of their adiyans, he continued, there would be no labour problem in Kuttanad today. It is significant that not a single agricultural labourer who was interviewed expressed such a view regarding the old system, although some conceded that it did give them a measure of security. Every worker expressed the view that it was a system that enslaved, oppressed, exploited, and degraded them. There is little doubt that whatever else may be said of the system, it encouraged the arbitrary exercise of power in which physical violence or the threat of it played no small part. While the landlords are nostalgic about the old system, the labourers have no regrets that it has changed so drastically and so fast.

WAGE RATES AND STANDARD OF LIVING

The assessment of the relative economic status of agricultural labourers is not an easy task. First of all, agricultural wages vary a great deal not only from region to region but also from village to village within the same region, and even within the same village. Secondly, to obtain real wage rates money wages must be deflated by a weighted consumer price index in the construction of which there seems to be no method accepted as completely satisfactory by economists.[19] Thirdly, even accurate real wage rates, calculated on a daily basis, cannot tell us much about changes in the annual wage rates of agricultural labourers if the quantum of work available is not taken into account—a point of considerable importance in Kuttanad. Fourthly, the relative position of the agricultural labourers can be gauged only if considered in comparison with other sectors of society, particularly the farmers. Finally, we must also take into account the changed social and cultural context which has created new needs and aspirations among the agricultural labourers.

There are a number of studies that attempt to determine the relative position in the 1960's of the lowest strata of Indian society, in particular, of agricultural labourers. In general, they present none too bright a picture. In a study of poverty in India Dandekar and Wrath concluded that between 1961-62 and 1967-68 per capita consumer expenditures among the bottom 5 per cent of villagers declined slightly while those of the rest of the bottom 20 per cent virtually stagnated. This was in contrast to the considerable improvement in consumer expenditures among the top 30 per cent of the population both in the villages and in the towns.[20] A number of specific studies of agricultural labourers came to the conclusion that during the 1960's agricultural wages declined in real terms in all states, with the notable exception of Kerala and Punjab/Haryana.[21] By updating and extending the study to 1971-72, A. V. Jose found that improvement in real wages took place also in Tamil Nadu, Uttar Pradesh, and Gujarat.[22] It is striking that Kerala emerged as a leader in this respect. In fact, Burdan's comparative study of wage rate movements in the Intensive Agricultural District Programme districts in various states between 1962-63 and 1967-68 concluded that real wage rates recorded the highest percentage increase in the Alleppey and Palghat districts of Kerala.[23] It should be noted, on the other hand, that the increase in agricultural production associated with the Green Revolution has been much greater in the IADP districts of other states such as Punjab, Tamil Nadu, and Gujarat. However, in a study of the wage rates of agricultural labourers in Kerala, A. V. Jose argued that the consumer price index used by Burdan and other earlier students was not satisfactory for Kerala. The use of an alternate consumer price index constructed by him showed that the rise in the real wage rate in Kerala between 1960-61 and 1967-68 may have been far lower than indicated by earlier studies.[24] Although Jose excluded Kuttanad from his study because of its peculiar features, his conclusion does raise questions about the reliability of the conclusions arrived at by the earlier authors.

The report of the Kuttanad Inquiry Commission gives some data on wage rates specifically for Kuttanad. Even this has many shortcomings as pointed out in the dissenting note by one of its members, the only professional economist in the commission.[25] It is nevertheless valuable and gives some information on money wage rates and paddy prices (see Table 15). It can be seen from the table that the paddy equivalent of the money wages of agricultural labourers declined steadily from 1944-45 to 1967-68. In 1969-70 and 1970-71 it showed some increase mainly because of the fall in the price of paddy. It is important to note that as late as 1969-70 the paddy equivalent of the daily money wage of a male agricultural labourer was below the level of 1944-45. In 1970-71 it increased by 8.7 per cent above the 1944-45 level. Table 16 gives the same data for the years 1971-72 to 1975-76. Unfortunately, the paddy prices for 1971-72 through 1973-74 are not provided. In 1974-75 the paddy equivalent of the male labourer's daily wage was again below the 1944-45 level, mainly because paddy prices reached a peak of Rs. 13 per para. In 1975-76 paddy prices were Rs. 10 per para and the paddy equivalent of the male labourer's daily wage rose to 7.2 kg. This was still only 26.3 per cent above the 1944-45 level.

TABLE 15: DAILY WAGE RATES, PADDY PRICES, AND THE PADDY EQUIVALENT OF DAILY WAGES IN KUTTANAD, 1944-45 TO 1970-71

Year	Daily Wage Rate per Male Worker (Rupees)	Farm Price of Paddy per Standard Para (Rupees)	Paddy Equivalent of Daily Wage of a Male Worker (Kilograms)
1944-45	1.37	1.75	5.7
1949-50	1.50	2.00	5.5
1954-55	1.56	2.00	5.6
1959-60	2.00	2.90	5.0
1964-65	2.75	5.65	3.5
1965-66	3.25	6.80	3.5
1966-67	3.75	8.70	3.1
1967-68	4.65	11.25	3.0
1968-69	4.65	8.25	4.1
1969-70	5.50	7.85	5.1
1970-71	6.00	7.00	6.2

Source: *Report of the Kuttanad Inquiry Commission,* p. 27

It is instructive to compare this data with the data collected from very knowledgeable informants during field work. Before World War Two, wages were paid almost entirely in kind in Kuttanad. In the early 1940's a male field labourer received 8 *kulians*[26] or one-half of a para of paddy as his daily wage and a female labourer received 5 kulians or one-third of a para of paddy. During the peak season wages tended to be higher, and a male labourer might receive as much as three-fourths or more of a para of paddy. If the normal wage rate of the early

TABLE 16: WAGE RATES, PADDY PRICES, AND PADDY EQUIVALENT OF DAILY
WAGES IN KUTTANAD, 1971-72 TO 1975-76

Year	Daily Wage Rates per Male Worker (Rupees)	Farm Price of Paddy per Standard Para (Rupees)	Paddy Equivalent of Daily Wage of a Male Worker (Kilograms)
1971-72	7.20	—	—
1972-73	8.50	—	—
1973-74	9.00	—	—
1974-75	10.00	13	5.6
1975-76	10.00	10	7.2

1940's is compared to the paddy equivalent of money wages in 1975, it is seen that in the latter year a male labourer received approximately three-fourths and a female labourer one-half of a para of paddy respectively, representing an increase of 50 per cent in both cases. The payment for harvesting was one-eleventh of the harvested paddy, known locally as *padam,* although this also varied considerably, rising to as much as one-sixth the share of harvested paddy in some areas. In 1975 it was fixed at one-seventh of the harvested paddy. If we compare this with the lowest rate in the early 1940's (apparently the most common) this represents an increase of 57.1 per cent. There was also the custom of paying *theerpu,*[27] a gift of paddy with each measure of padam. Today this is fixed as one-fourth of the padam, that is, one-fourth of one-seventh of the harvested paddy.

The conclusion that must be drawn from the foregoing discussion is that the rise in the daily wage rates of agricultural labourers in Kuttanad, if any, has been quite modest even after the coming of the Green Revolution and much less striking than has been generally supposed. This is not the whole story, however. What rise there has been in wage rates seems to have been almost completely offset by the rise in unemployment. Unfortunately, precise data relating to the increase in unemployment among the agricultural labourers of Kuttanad are not available. Agricultural Labour Inquiries of 1950-51 and 1956-57 give us the number of unemployed days per worker in various states in India. Table 17 shows that Kerala has not only the highest incidence of unemployment among agricultural labourers but also one of the highest rates of increase with respect to such incidence of unemployment (45 days per worker). The figures given by the Minimum Wages Committee for Employment in Agriculture of the government of Travancore-Cochin in 1956 were remarkably similar. According to their report, a male worker got, on the average, work for 201 days during the year and a female worker 131 days.[28] Evidently Kuttanad would be one of the worst-hit areas in the state. Fortunately, the Kuttanad Inquiry Commission collected some data on unemployment among agricultural labourers. It estimated that in 1971 a male worker in Kuttanad got only 100 to 120 days of work and a female worker only 80 to 100 days of work.[29] Agricultural labour leaders in Kuttanad say that even this is an overestimate. Taking into account these unemployment figures, an estimate can be made of the changes in the mean annual wage of a male agricultural labourer in Kuttanad. As is clear from Table 18, despite some fluctuations the annual wage of a male agricultural worker in Kuttanad in the 1970's was substantially lower than that in the 1950's. In fact, the average for the 1970's (760) is 37.9 percent lower than the average for the 1950's (1223), and the figure for 1975 is 34.5 percent below the 1950 level.

TABLE 17: UNEMPLOYMENT OF ADULT MALE CASUAL AND ATTACHED WORKERS, 1950-51 AND 1956-57 (NUMBER OF UNEMPLOYED DAYS PER WORKER)

	Casual Adult Male Workers		Attached Adult Male Workers	
States	1950-51	1956-57	1950-51	1956-57
Andra Pradesh	132	126	8	12
Assam	71	94	12	67
Bihar	85	120	21	119
Bombay	137	113	12	38
Karnataka	98	118	38	79
Kerala	125	170	138	145
Madhya Pradesh	77	117	12	45
Orissa	53	135	7	43
Punjab	155	150	41	32
Rajasthan	99	138	19	39
Tamilnadu	107	162	24	68
Uttar Pradesh	48	124	11	69
West Bengal	93	113	17	47
All India	90	128	19	68

Can the wages of the agricultural labourers have fallen so drastically during the first twenty-five years of the country's independence despite what appears to be successful trade unionism? If they have, only a few older agricultural labourers and some of the more perceptive communist leaders in Kuttanad seem to be aware of this fact. It may be that this manner of calculating the real average annual wages does not give an accurate picture of the situation. It is also possible that despite the loss of workdays the workers' incomes have increased as a result of their being granted house sites or of other casual employment, such as illegal processing of paddy. It also seems likely that the wages for earlier years have

TABLE 18: NUMBER OF DAYS OF EMPLOYMENT, PADDY EQUIVALENT OF DAILY WAGES, AND PADDY EQUIVALENT OF MEAN ANNUAL WAGE OF MALE WORKERS IN KUTTANAD, 1950-1975

Year	Number of Days of Employment[1]	Paddy Equivalent of Daily Wages of a Male Worker (in kgs)	Mean Annual Wage of a Male Worker in Kuttanad (in kgs of Paddy)
1950	240	5.5	1320
1956	201	5.6[2]	1126
1971	120	6.2	744
1974	120[3]	5.6	672
1975	120[3]	7.2	864

[1] Note that the number of working days for 1950 is for Kerala and that for 1956 for Travancore-Cochin.

[2] This figure is for 1954-55.

[3] The 1971 figures have been used for 1974 and 1975. If anything, the number of days of employment would have declined, not increased since that year.

Source: Tables II, III, IV and Government of Travancore-Cochin, *Report of the Minimum Wages Committee for Employment in Agriculture,* 1956

been overestimated. The apparently higher annual wages may have been offset by perpetual indebtedness and interest payments and, more importantly (a point which will be illustrated in Chapter 5), by the fact that the full amount of the annual wages were, in reality, seldom paid to the workers. When all these caveats have been stated, however, the evidence is still impressive enough to suggest some decline or, at the very least, stagnation in the average, real annual incomes of Kuttanad's agricultural labourers. Is there, then, no substance to the much talked about union successes, wage increases, and agricultural labour prosperity? It seems that at least part of the answer to the question must be sought in the increasing internal differentiation among the agricultural workers. In the last chapter mention was made of an emerging group of upwardly mobile agricultural labourers and small peasants who are acquiring land and becoming landowners. It seems certain that some agricultural labour families have prospered and that these are the ones fortunate enough to have steady employment, more than average number of able-bodied workers in the family, and, above all, additional or alternative sources of income. These families are also likely to be found among the Ezhavas rather than the Harijans. If this is true, it is clear that the average annual incomes and consequently the living standards of the rest of the workers, of the majority, have deteriorated in both relative and absolute terms.

So far, this discussion has focussed on the economic position of agricultural labourers in relation to their position in the past. It is also necessary to look at their position relative to that of the other major sector in the agricultural population, the farmers. The economic position of the farmers will not be examined here in any detail. In addition to the discussion regarding this in the last two chapters, it will be sufficient to state that the income and the standard of living of the farmers have increased substantially since the 1940's, particularly since the early 1960's. Even if the real incomes of agricultural labourers have increased in proportion to those of the farmers, it is clear that the gap between the two must have increased enormously in absolute terms. After all, the gap between 1,000 rupees and 100,000 rupees is much wider than that between 100 rupees and 10,000 rupees. Never before has so much rural wealth been displayed in Kuttanad as today, and never before have so many luxury goods found their way into Kuttanad.

There is one further point that needs to be considered here. This concerns the changed social and cultural context in which today's agricultural labourers live and the new needs and aspirations this has created, in particular those aspects of the change that have had an impact on their consumer expenditure and have made demands on their meagre incomes. Earlier in this chapter an old politician in Kuttanad was quoted as remarking that the agricultural labourers had only two needs, namely, to have a roof over their heads and to fill their bellies. He was correct, at least to an extent. To be sure, they had a few other needs—a few items of clothing, a few straw mats, some pots and pans. But they rarely bought these for money. Old clothes could be collected from the master's house, and mats could be woven in their spare time. Most of their wages would be spent on food. There was not much else they could think of buying anyway. Today, this has completely changed. It is only a rare Pulaya labourer in Kuttanad who will now collect old clothes from the landlord's house; none will collect the leftovers from the landlord's plates or plantain leaves after a feast, just as none will allow himself to be insulted or abused by a landlord. All these are considered degrading. Today the agricultural labourer in Kuttanad takes special care and pride in appearing clean, well dressed, and well groomed. And many of the women even attempt to be fashionable. This means that they spend a good deal of money on clothes, toilet soaps, and even cosmetics. Lux soap and talcum powder, pocket mirrors and combs have been added to the list of their consumer items. It seems that they are determined never again to allow themselves to be insulted for being ''dirty and uncouth.'' There are also other needs which are even more important. Almost every child between the ages of five and sixteen is in school, a few older ones in college. As members of scheduled castes most of them do not pay tuition, and many receive small stipends from the government. Nevertheless, education is an expensive commodity; books, umbrellas, proper clothes, all require money. New forms of entertainment are also attracting the attention of agricultural labourers, and these too are costly. The cinema is everywhere within walking distance and is the one cultural item on which most money is spent.

These consumer habits are seen by many people as signs of prosperity among the agricultural labourers. But it is likely that they are meeting these new needs, which they now consider absolutely essential, by cutting expenditures elsewhere. Some labourers and labour leaders report that the pattern of food consumption has deteriorated both in quantity and quality over the years. "After all," said one labour leader, "no one sees your empty stomach. You can always tighten your *dhoti* and walk with your head high; it is by your appearance that people judge you." There is little doubt that these consumer habits and attitudes among the agricultural labourers are signs of profound cultural changes. The landlords have a word for it—arrogance; labourers and their leaders call it a new sense of dignity; from the point of view of a sociologist, perhaps the best way to describe it is as a new collective consciousness which is by no means unrelated to politics or to agrarian conflicts.

RURAL PROLETARIANS

It is evident that the relationship of the agricultural labourers to their employers and to land, the means of production, has changed profoundly, as has also the normative order governing this relationship. What securities the labourers enjoyed in the past, what personal interest they took in cultivating the land of their masters, what loyalty and personal bonds existed between them and their employers, have gone forever. Today they are wage labourers, proletarians. But they are rural proletarians, agriculturalists without land. And this has profound implications in the changing contexts of Kerala and India. Landlessness places them in a peculiar situation in relation to the structural changes and rural development programmes initiated by various governments. Distribution of land to the landless has never been an important aim of land reform anywhere in India. The Green Revolution and other possible achievements in rural development benefit the farmers with land. They can benefit the landless labourers only to the extent to which they get translated into increased wages. It is under these conditions that the labourers also face mounting unemployment, the effects of which have already been discussed.

It must also be noted that agricultural labourers still do not enjoy many benefits enjoyed by their counterparts in industry. They receive no bonuses, paid holidays, maternity benefits, or overtime payments. Under present conditions their lives may be more insecure and alienating than those of the industrial workers. As one local labour leader said, even factory workers have some permanent relationship both to the factory and to their tools. For instance, it is not uncommon for a labourer to apply grease to his tools before leaving the factory at the end of the day. But the casual agricultural labourers must wander from place to place searching for work. These facts about the lives of the agricultural labourers of Kuttanad must be kept in mind throughout the consideration of their movement and struggles in the following chapter.

$$5$$

Organization and Struggle

SOCIAL AND POLITICAL BACKGROUND

The awakening and the organization of the agricultural labourers of Kuttanad were greatly facilitated by the social and political developments in Travancore in general and in Alleppey in particular. The first half of this century saw three types of interrelated movements that shook the quiet life of the people of Kerala. These were the Social Reform Movements, the Nationalist and Political Movements, and the Trade Union Movements. Some aspects of the Social Reform Movements, which mainly took the form of Caste Associations, have already been described. By 1920 every important caste in Kerala had its caste association which had two major aims: first, to improve its position *vis-à-vis* other castes, and second, to modernize the caste internally. It has been seen how in the process the caste associations attacked untouchability and various other forms of caste discrimination and contributed to a general awakening, especially among the lower castes. This chapter will be concerned mainly with the two other movements in which Alleppey played a very important role.

Unlike the Social Reform Movements which took hold earlier and more firmly in Travancore, the anti-colonial and nationalist movement developed earlier in Malabar. This was only natural because Malabar was a district of the Madras Presidency of British India while Travancore was a princely state, and the Indian National Congress had confined its activities mainly to the British area. When the movement finally came to Travancore, however, it took as militant and radical a form as it did in Malabar. By the early 1930's a cleavage between the right and the left had become clearly visible within the Indian Nationalist movement, and in 1935 the left formed the Congress Socialist Party

(CSP). From the beginning, Kerala (Malabar and the two princely states of Travancore and Cochin) was among the few regions in India where the left took firm roots. Working within the Congress, the militants of the left travelled throughout Kerala, establishing contact with like-minded people, founding libraries, and organizing trade unions, Youth Leagues, and Study Classes.[1]

Meanwhile, Alleppey had already emerged as a hotbed of trade union and radical activities. The first Labour Organization in Kerala had been founded in Alleppey in 1922 under the name of the Travancore Labour Association. Founded as an association of the workers of the Empire Coir Works in Alleppey by a yard superintendent and foreman, it soon became the organization of the workers of all the coir factories of Alleppey. When the Travancore Trade Union Act came into effect in 1938, it became the first trade union to be registered under the act with the registration No. 1 under the name of the Travancore Coir Factory Workers Union. This organization was to play a crucial role in spreading the message of the trade union movement and of the revolution all over Travancore and in training a cadre of able and dedicated workers for the cause of trade unionism and the revolutionary movement. Under the leadership of P. Keshav Dev, a Communist who was to become a well-known writer in Malayalam, the Labour Association in 1925-26 organized the first strike ever to occur in Alleppey. The Association not only grew in militancy and strength but soon became very politicized as the CSP, and later the Communist Party, became its patron and parent organization. A branch of the CSP was established in Alleppey, and leaders of the Party in Malabar maintained constant contact with the union workers in Alleppey. By the early 1940's it was difficult to find a coir factory or any other industrial enterprise in the two taluks of Ambalapuzha (in which were both Alleppey and Kuttanad) and Shertallai where a trade union had not been established. Unions had been organized among port workers, tile workers, textile workers, cashew workers, paper mill workers, head-load workers, *beedi* (local cigarette) workers, fishermen, toddy tappers, coconut tree climbers, and boatmen. It seems that the union organizers who believed in the leading role of the industrial proletariat in revolution did not turn to the organization of agricultural workers until they had exhausted all the other sectors of the working class. The All Travancore Trade Union Congress (ATTUC) had also come into existence by the early 1940's.

It was no secret that the CSP in Kerala was a party of radicals and Communists. When a branch of the Indian Communist Party was formally established in Travancore in 1940 the CSP members joined it *en bloc*. Under the leadership of the Party and the unions, regular classes were organized for the workers and their leaders in which they were given training in English, elocution, and the principles of Marxism. How remarkable this training programme must have been can be inferred from the fact that it transformed at least a dozen semi-literate workers into leaders who went on to assume various political and administrative offices as well as becoming good public speakers and even writers. It should not be surprising that these organizations were not mere trade unions and that their demands were not just economic. This is clearly borne out from the nature of the struggles they organized, especially the general strike of 1938 and the uprising in Punnapra and Vayalar in 1946.

The general strike organized by the Coir Factory Workers Union in 1938 was the first of its kind in the history of Kerala. All over Travancore a campaign had been under way for ending the autocratic rule of the Raja and the *divan* (minister or aide) and demanding "responsible government." In this campaign both the CSP and the Coir Factory Workers Union joined the State Congress.[2] The union began an indefinite strike demanding, among other things, immediate acceptance by the government of adult franchise, freeing of political prisoners, and increased wages. In a demonstration organized by the State Congress in front of the Raja's palace, twenty-five "red volunteers" from Alleppey participated. In Alleppey, rallies and demonstrations were held defying a police ban, the participants laying themselves open to ruthless police repression. The strike lasted twenty-five days. The union and the Communists had acquired a number of martyrs. Although the state did not get a "responsible government," the workers won a wage increase of 6.25 per cent and had their jailed leaders freed. The workers and the organizers of the strike saw it as a great success. It was an event that boosted the morale of the workers immensely.

If the political processes were thus leading to the awakening of the agricultural workers of Kuttanad, the economic crisis brought about by the depression and the war seemed to make their organization and struggle a matter of urgency. The prices of essential commodities shot up enormously in the whole state of Travancore. There was a crisis in the supply of rice, the staple of the state. Imports from Burma, which had filled the state's deficit and fed its people, stopped arriving as the Burmese border became closed. As a consequence the price of paddy increased sharply. Determined to draw the maximum profit from the crisis, the landlords began substituting the prevailing paddy wages with cash for all the agricultural operations except harvesting. This represented a drastic reduction in the real wages of the workers. According to S. K. Das, an early organizer of the agricultural labour union, with one para of paddy the landlords were now able to pay as many as ten female workers whereas before the change they paid only three female workers with the same amount. With skyrocketing prices, decreased wages, and essential commodities in short supply, the suffering and discontent among the agricultural workers increased.[3] The agricultural workers of Kuttanad, it seemed, were waiting to be organized.

RISE OF TRADE UNIONISM AMONG AGRICULTURAL LABOURERS

Given the geographical and ecological conditions of Alleppey and its surrounding areas the impact of the trade union and political developments in Alleppey could not have failed to be felt in Kuttanad. Interaction between Alleppey and the surrounding areas is intense. Moreover, coir factories and coir factory workers are spread all over the coastal areas. A large number of coir workers were drawn from Kuttanad whose relatives were still agricultural workers in many cases. The general strike of 1938 seems to have made a great impression on the minds of many workers and young men in Kuttanad as elsewhere. It was in this context that the idea of unionizing the agricultural workers arose in the minds of some people.

As may be expected, the initiative came from radical and trade union activists in Alleppey. Perhaps they were moved by the sufferings of the agricultural labourers. Or, perhaps they had exhausted all organizable types of industrial workers. An annual issue of a labour union magazine in the late 1930's carried an article by V. K. Pururshottaman dealing with the many problems of agricultural labourers. Towards the end of 1939 a meeting was convened by S. K. Das in the village of Pallathuruthy in which about fifty agricultural labourers participated.[4] It was not long before the *Travancore Karshaka Thozhilali Union* (Travancore Agricultural Labour Union) came into being with T. K. Varghese Vaidyan as president and S. K. Das as secretary. Soon the activities of the union spread to such places as Kainakari and Kavalam. Its initial major demand was that the old mode of paying wages in kind be re-established. Many coir factory union activists from Alleppey travelled throughout Kuttanad mobilizing agricultural labourers. Those who lost their regular wages on such occasions were supported by their co-workers in their departments who contributed a share of their daily wages for this purpose. Initially Kainakari was made the headquarters of the union. In the early 1950's it moved to Mamkompu, the present headquarters of the Kuttanad taluk.

The growth of the agricultural labour movement in Kuttanad has been spectacular. During the past three decades the movement grew to be a very strong and militant force organizing many struggles—strikes, boycotts, and land grab movements—and, as a result, coming into confrontation with the landlords, their agents, and the police. By the time of the great Punnapra-Vayalar uprising in 1946 (see p. 000), the movement had spread not only to all parts of Kuttanad, but to the entire region comprising the two taluks of Ambalapuzha and Shertallai. It is important to note that unions were organized at local and grass-roots levels, and that local organizations functioned relatively independently although in close touch with their parent bodies, the local party units. More centralized organizations at the state and even district level appear to be a recent development. Hence, although the TKTU dominated most of Kuttanad, there were also other unions led by the same Communist Party.

The success of the Communist Party in building a strong base among the agricultural labourers of Kuttanad caught the attention of the other political parties in the area. It was not long before they were all in the field competing for the loyalty of the workers. The Indian National Congress established a branch of their trade union, the Indian National Trade Union Congress (INTUC), in Kuttanad in 1954. However, it never really got off the ground and fell into disarray very soon. It was not until 1970 that a nationwide organization, the *Desiya Karshaka Thozhilali Union* (National Agricultural Labour Union) came into existence under the auspices of the new Congress Party led by Indira Gandhi. Around the same time, a branch of the union became active in Alleppey district. At present its membership does not exceed four or five thousand and is drawn predominantly from such specialized groups of workers as ploughmen and motor operators. In terms of caste, there is little Harijan presence among its membership, which is predominantly upper caste (Christian, Nair, and Ezhava). Another party in the field is the Revolutionary Socialist Party (RSP) which organized the *Kuttanad Karshaka Thozhilali Union* (KKTU) in 1968. It initiated the movement with the avowed aim of "facing the Marxist menace."[5] This organization, however, has little significance in Kuttanad—its membership is not more than a few hundred—and its presence and activities are confined to some isolated areas within Kuttanad.

It may be noted that the rise of agricultural labour unions led also to the organization of farmers' associations. Although farmers' associations had existed in Kuttanad since the late 1930's they were little more than clubs of big landlords which engaged in lobbying the bureaucrats and politicians for predominantly economic concessions, such as subsidies for pumping and agricultural implements. The *Kuttanad Karshaka Sangham* (KKS) which came into existence in the lower Kuttanad area in 1939, for instance, remained exclusive and unresponsive to the needs of middle farmers as late as 1957. By contrast, the more militant and active organizations came into existence as a direct response to the threat posed by the Communist-led labour unions. The most militant of these has been the *Upper Kuttanad Karshaka Sangham* (UKKS) which was established between 1957 and 1959 when the CPI was in power in Kerala. It had its origin in the "Democratic Sangh," a para-military force organized by militant anti-communists in the Tiruvalla area, which is dominated by middle-class Christians and is well known for its political conservatism. By the early 1960's the various farmers' associations had been co-ordinated under a federating organization, the *Akhila Kuttanad Karshaka Sangham* (All Kuttanad Farmers' Association or AKKS). This organization has been sponsored by the Kerala Congress, a dissident group which broke away from the Congress Party in Kerala in 1964 and which predominantly represents the interests of middle- and upper-class Syrian Christians and, to a limited extent, of Nairs. In 1972 the KKS claimed a membership of about 3,500 and the UKKS 9,000.

It should be pointed out here that both the CPI and the CPI(M) have sponsored their own farmers' associations. Of these the CPI(M)-sponsored *Kerala Karshaka Sangham* is the more important one with a membership of about 10,000. Both draw their membership predominantly from marginal and small peasants. Neither of them, however, has any significant impact on the agrarian scene in Kuttanad, and neither of them engages in any conflict with agricultural labourers.

PATTERNS OF STRUGGLE

The fact that the agricultural labour movement in Kuttanad was largely a front of the Communist Party [first the CPI and then the CPI(M)] meant that its policies, strategies, and fortunes were tied up with those of its parent organization. It is well known that the Communist Party's policies and strategies are not necessarily determined by local conditions or factors; they are often affected by national and international developments. It should not be surprising, therefore, that the patterns of struggle organized by the agricultural labour union have fluctuated greatly and passed through many phases. As will be seen later, since the early 1970's it has entered its latest phase of class collaboration, virtually discontinuing its militant struggles and bringing to Kuttanad a peace that it has not seen in three decades.

The first thirteen years of the movement, from 1938 to 1951, were a difficult and trying period. It was no easy task to persuade the workers to overcome their fear and to come out openly to join the union and to participate in struggles. It must also be kept in mind that between 1946 and 1951 both the union and the Party functioned as illegal organizations following the Punnapra-Vayalar uprising. Initially the union organizers found it impossible to attract Pulaya workers into the movement. Those who joined the union became victims of various forms of repression—beatings, loss of employment, false lawsuits, and eviction from their homesteads.

One of the early organizers of the union described the first instance of a struggle involving Pulaya labourers in 1943. It involved sixteen attached labourers of four important landlord families who cultivated a large padasekharam in the D block kayal. An attached labourer generally received an initial advance payment of ten paras of paddy and several instalments of payments during the course of the year, the total supposedly amounting to one hundred paras. However, it was always the landlord who kept the accounts, and when they were settled at the end of the year the labourer often found that he was in debt. A typical labourer found himself owing eight to nine paras of paddy to the landlord. He would then hear the landlord ask casually, "what are you doing next year?" "Where, my thampran," he would reply, "can your slave go?" "Well, then," the landlord would say, "here is the balance of your advance for next year, two paras of paddy." Thus, not only could the labourer never get out of debt, but also he seldom received more than a small portion of his yearly advance and of his yearly wage. In the particular instance referred to above, the sixteen workers decided to approach the union leaders, complaining that they had been unable to receive any adequate compensation for their year's work. The union leaders approached the employers, and a process of bargaining and mutual threats followed. It ended in a victory for the union. Faced with the threat of an all-out strike involving the union leaders, who had already become known and influential in the area, the landlords capitulated and agreed to re-examine the yearly accounts of the sixteen workers. The result was that all the sixteen workers received payments ranging between forty-six and eighty-seven paras of paddy. It appears that the event created a stir among the Pulaya labourers and was a turning point in the history of the agricultural labour movement in Kuttanad. The sixteen Pulaya workers were members of kinship, caste, and church groups. The Church Mission Society[6] churches in the area to which they and many other neo-Christian converts belonged became active centres of the movement, and they even received support from the local church leaders who were their own caste men.

In the initial years of the movement women workers proved to be more active and militant than their menfolk. During the first ten years most struggles seem to have occurred during the two agricultural operations which mainly involve women, transplanting and harvesting. There were instances in which landlords were surrounded by women workers in the threshing fields and not allowed to leave the spot until they consented to the workers' demands, usually for higher wages. In one instance which took place in the 1940's, an important landlord in Kuttanad was tied with ropes and paddy was taken away by the workers forcibly. The men remained in the background; they felt too dependent on their thamprans to confront them openly. After all, except for the transplanting and harvesting seasons they were the principal workers and the main breadwinners in their households. It may also be noted that both men and women workers were much more militant and fearless when they were facing an unknown landlord in a village other than their own. It must be remembered that the agricultural labourer still maintained some personal relationship with his thampran and would perhaps have been completely intimidated at the prospect of a personal confrontation.

The most militant and violent struggle ever to be organized in Travancore under the auspices of the Communist Party and its front organizations was what has since become known as "Punnapra-Vayalar." The centres of the revolution were two villages, Punnapra and Vayalar, on the southern and northern fringes of Alleppey, respectively. More than anything else, this event seems to have contributed to a mass awakening among various sections of the population in the two taluks of Ambalapuzha and Shertallai. Agricultural Labour organizations had just become active in the two taluks when the abortive revolution took place in 1946. Confrontations between agricultural labourers and the landlord's thugs seem to have provided at least part of the background for the uprising, especially in and around Shertallai. Although the coir factory workers played the leading role in the revolt, there is no doubt that many agricultural labourers participated in it. The attempt to call it a peasant revolt is, therefore, not altogether without foundation.

In 1946, as India approached independence, the fate of the princely states remained uncertain. British plans for independence had left the future of the approximately five hundred princely states in the hands of the autocratic princes. In Travancore, the campaign for "responsible government" gained momentum again as the notorious divan, Sir C. P. Ramaswamy Aiyer ("C.P.") unveiled plans for constitutional reforms. His proposed "American Model" constitution envisaged a government in which a fixed and irremovable executive composed of the Raja and the divan (C.P. himself) would co-exist with an elected body of representatives and a cabinet. It seems that the divan had hoped to keep Travancore out of the Indian union with himself exercising real power in the independent state. When the State Congress, after some initial hesitation, expressed its willingness to enter into negotiations with C.P. on the proposed constitution, the Communists and the trade unions rejected it outright and planned to organize state-wide agitations, including a general strike for "responsible government." Meanwhile, there was much economic discontent in the taluks of Ambalapuzha and Shertallai. Shertallai had been the area in Kerala worst hit by the famine of 1943 that raged in various parts of India. According to an estimate made by the Servants of India Society, the famine had claimed roughly 21,000 victims in this taluk.[7] Needless to say, the situation was helpful to the organizers of the revolt.

The government of Sir C. P. Ramaswamy Aiyer prepared to face the threat with a combination of the carrot and the stick. First, it unleashed a reign of repression aimed especially against organized labour, both industrial and agricultural. Shertallai was made the centre of these repressive measures. This area had a number of big landlords who had become angered at the new activities of the agricultural labourers, and provided full support to the government, offering even their residences and other buildings for use as police and army camps. It is alleged by the workers that with the full knowledge and support of the police officers and the landlords, organized groups of thugs roamed through the villages beating up labour leaders, looting, raping, and burning red flags planted in front of the offices of the labour unions. The All Travancore Trade Union Congress (ATTUC) expressed its protest against these by organizing a one-day general strike. In October 1946, C.P. called a tripartite conference at which he offered the ATTUC representatives what is said to have been an attractive economic package, as well as representation in parliament, on condition that the unions accept his proposed constitutional reforms and call off their political agitations. The offer was rejected. Within days after this the two taluks of Ambalapuzha and Shertallai were filled with units of the police, the reserve police, and the army, who set up camps at various centres throughout the region.

The Communist Party and the ATTUC answered the government by setting up their own "people's camps" which were guarded by armed volunteers. These camps, set up at various centres in the two taluks, were led by trade councils representing many kinds of workers. The five camps in Shertallai alone had a total of 2,378 volunteers. The volunteers were given military training by ex-service-men and were armed with country weapons, mostly *varikundams* (spears made out of arecanut tree stems). They were given political lessons by leaders of the ATTUC and the Communist Party. It may be noted here that these developments took place not only with the full knowledge and approval of the Travancore and Kerala leadership, but also with the approval of the highest leadership of the Communist Party of India.[8]

The general strike which began on 22 October 1946 was a great success. The third day of the strike, 25 October, was the Maharaja's birthday on which the new constitution was to be implemented. The strike committee organized four huge demonstrations. The participants marched, shouting slogans and carrying red flags mounted on varikundams. One group of demonstrators attacked a relatively small police camp in the village of Punnapra, resulting in the death of a number of policemen and demonstrators. Following this, C.P. declared military rule in the state and proclaimed himself Lieutenant-Colonel. The army attacked most of the major volunteers' camps with machine guns and quelled the revolt within a few days. The worst firing took place in Vayalar near Shertallai on 27 October. On that day more than one hundred and fifty revolutionary fighters are reported to have fallen dead in that camp. The camps were soon dispersed and the general strike was called off on 31 October. More than sixty organizations in the state, including the ATTUC and the Communist Party, were banned. Many leaders and participants of the revolt were jailed and tortured, many went underground, and the movement seemed to have been crushed for the time being. Three persons, sentenced to death, later received pardon from the free Indian government. Most prisoners connected with the incident remained in jail until 1954, when they were freed by the United Front government headed by the Praja Socialist Party that had come to power in Travancore-Cochin[9] with Communist support.

Hardly a year after the seemingly crushing defeat, the Communist movement in Travancore was resurrected with renewed vigour and enthusiasm. Truly, the blood of its martyrs seemed to give it new life. In the 1950's, and to some extent as late as the split in the party in 1964, the Communist Party was the envy of all, including its enemies, for its organization, discipline, sense of dedication, hard work, and above all, incorruptibility. It penetrated all sections of society and was particularly successful in attracting to its fold a large proportion of the intellectuals of the state—writers, journalists, poets, playwrights, and artists of all kinds. They carried on a relentless campaign to create a body of revolutionary art and literature that dealt with the life of the common man in place of the characters of ancient mythology, of kings and their courtiers. ''Punnapra-Vayalar'' and its martyrs became part of their resources. The Kerala People's Arts Club (KPAC) which came into existence in the early 1950's gained great influence throughout the state. There can be no doubt that all this had considerable impact on the people of the state, particularly among those of Alleppey and Kuttanad.

When many cadres went underground after the suppression of the revolts,

Kuttanad became one of their favourite hiding places. Naturally, they came into direct contact with agricultural labourers who are reported to have harboured and protected them. It appears that the party directed these activists to make full use of this opportunity and to devote their time and energy to the agricultural labour front. Many a meeting is said to have been held in the kayals and canals of Kuttanad in country boats with roofs, rowed by local agricultural labourers. Party activists claim that the seemingly quiet and uneventful period of preparation was important in the rapid advance of the movement in the area.

In 1951 the party and its front organizations became legal, and the activists came out from hiding and began working openly. Between 1951 and 1957 the union organized a number of protests which won it prestige and helped it to consolidate its strength. Two struggles in particular deserve to be mentioned here. Both were directed against well-known and influential individuals, and both ended in the victory of the union. They not only enhanced the union's prestige, but helped agricultural labourers to liberate themselves from the fear and subservience that had oppressed their minds for so long.

The first of these struggles took place in 1954 and was against Murickan, the biggest of Kuttanad's landlords. The issue was wages. The union demanded three *edanghazhis*[10] paddy as the daily wage of a female labourer. Murickan refused to comply with the workers' demand. The workers struck, and simultaneously one hundred volunteers staged a satyagraha (non-violent protest) in front of the landlord's residence. The residence is on the bank of the Pumpa River, and when the police refused to let the workers enter the compound, they staged the satyagraha in boats in the river in front of the residence. The strike and the satyagraha lasted eighteen days. In the end, the landlord agreed to abide by the decision of a government-sponsored conference, and the decision was in favour of the workers. Most of the landlord's workers who participated in the struggle belonged to the village of Kumarakom in Kottayam district a few miles away. It is reported that the entire families of the hundred volunteers had set up camps in Kavalam, the site of the struggle, and did not return to their native village of Kumarakom until the conclusion of the struggle.

The second struggle occurred in the fields of an ex-cabinet minister in the government of Travancore-Cochin. Here the issue was theerpu, the ''gift'' of paddy sheaves given to the workers at harvest time. K. M. Kora, who had just returned to Kuttanad after leaving his cabinet post, refused to pay the theerpu. The workers struck demanding one theerpu for two days of harvesting—the customary amount. Kora sent for the police, who arrested and jailed more than seventy workers. Several of the leaders were also taken into custody. In the meantime the landlord attempted to harvest his paddy with the help of outside workers. To prevent this union volunteers picketed the fields; they too were arrested and jailed. In the end the workers won their demand, but it was a costly struggle; the police are said to have been brutal and to have tortured the workers and the union leaders, breaking the ribs of one of the leaders. The union leaders allege that the ex-minister used his personal influence to have the police use un-usually brutal measures in the hope of crushing the labour movement.

The first election in the newly formed state of Kerala brought the Communist Party to power in 1957. This had considerable impact on the agrarian situation in Kuttanad. The new labour minister was the veteran Communist leader from Alleppey, T. V. Thomas. The government appointed a committee to investigate minimum wages for agricultural labourers. It also called a high-level tripartite conference to define the guidelines and set up the necessary structure for settling agrarian conflicts. Out of this was born the Industrial Relations Committee (IRC) for Kuttanad, a tripartite body established in July 1957. Prior to 1957, in situations of agrarian disputes the landlords were able to call upon the police to take their side against the workers. But the new government took immediate steps to restrain the police from interfering in industrial and agrarian disputes as partisans for the management or owners. It is possible that the Communist-led workers and their local leaders saw this as a good opportunity to wrest hitherto-denied concessions from their employers. In any case, conflicts in Kuttanad increased in both number and intensity. Landlords, particularly in the upper Kuttanad area, began organizing para-military *sanghams,* or "fronts," and groups of thugs to confront the organized strength of the workers. It is quite probable, however, that these organizations came into existence not simply in response to the increased militancy of the agricultural labourers, but to the more general "Communist threat" in the state.[11] The most prominent among these was the "Democratic *Sangh.*" In the upper Kuttanad area dominated by the sangh a group of Pulayas allegedly attacked a Syrian Christian farmer and his family while the latter were harvesting paddy in their field. In any case, hundreds of armed Christians attacked the Pulayas in the area, disabling many and killing some.

Between 1957 and 1959 the union made several demands, and some of these led to large-scale violence. In 1957 the union demanded an increase in the payment for harvesting from one-eleventh to one-ninth of the harvested paddy. When the farmers refused to concede the demand the workers struck. The farmers tried to do the harvesting with loyal workers, usually brought from outside. This was opposed by the workers and ended in physical confrontation and violence. In 1958 the union's demands were mainly two—increase in the wage rates and reduction in the hours of work from eight to six in the punja fields and to five in the kayal fields. The farmers accepted the first demand, but refused to accept the second. However, the union fixed the working hours unilaterally from nine to twelve in the morning and two to five in the afternoon. The union's representatives were to announce the time to begin and to end work by a showing of the red flag. Nothing could have been more humiliating to the landlords. But for the time being, at least, there was little they could do except to watch helplessly the erosion of their control and its replacement by that of the union representatives. Soon the farmers' association took the matter to the IRC; after persistent pressure from the association and prolonged discussions the IRC finally arrived at a decision to replace the red flag with sirens to be installed in convenient centres in Kuttanad and to be controlled and operated by the *Panchayat,* or village-level government.

From the late 1950's it is possible to discern a regular pattern in the struggles of the agricultural labourers. Almost every agricultural season the union makes a number of demands, pressing them if necessary with strikes or other forms of struggle. The farmers may attempt to resist the union's demands. Where and when the farmers are well organized or a landlord is resourceful enough to assemble a group of hirelings and thugs, a physical confrontation would follow, resulting in violence and often in police interference. In many cases, however, farmers simply accede to the demands of the union. Finally, an IRC meeting is convened from which a compromise settlement is likely to emerge. In arriving at these settlements the "established facts" resulting from the union's struggle are always taken into account. The IRC would, for instance, seldom reduce a certain rate of wage that the farmers have already begun to pay. It may be observed here that in the physical confrontations and violence the larger farmers very rarely participate personally; more often than not it would be their hirelings and thugs who would do the physical fighting. By contrast, the union leaders personally lead the struggles. The rank of the leader of a struggle will depend on the extent and prestige value of the particular struggle. Some of the larger and more prestigious struggles have been led by the district-level president of the union.

The use of tractors became an issue in Kuttanad in 1962. Since the late 1950's some of the wealthier farmers in Kuttanad were attempting to introduce tractors in an effort to make cultivation more efficient and, it would seem, more importantly, to get rid of some of their troublesome workers. This attempt, however, met with violent opposition from the *Kuttanad Taluka Uzhavv Thozhilali* (Ploughmen's) *Union,* a CPI(M)-led organization that operates as a wing of the KSKTU. The union introduced a resolution in the IRC in 1962 to ban the use of tractors in Kuttanad. As prolonged discussions and arguments went on within the IRC, the union activists made it very clear that the use of tractors would be impossible in practice without their co-operation. Their strategy was to plough the landlords' fields by force, even after these had been ploughed with tractors. Many landlords were thus forced to pay wages to their former customary ploughmen whose work was neither useful nor requested by them. It was not until 1969 that the IRC made a final decision regarding this, which has been respected since then to a large extent. Accordingly, any farmer in Kuttanad may now use tractor ploughing subject to the condition that wherever such ploughing is done, one round of additional cattle ploughing should be done in the case of kayal lands and two rounds of cattle ploughing in the case of karappadams, so as to avoid unemployment among the ploughers.

One of the most significant events affecting the agricultural labour movement in Kuttanad was the split between the Rightists and the Leftists within the CPI in 1964 on the fundamental question of approaches to the Congress Party.[12] The

Right Communists (Communist Party of India or CPI) give critical support to the Congress Party and unequivocally support the USSR (which gives aid to the Congress government), and they hope for a peaceful transition to a national democratic state led jointly by the bourgeoisie and the workers. The Left Communists, Communist Party of India (Marxist) or CPI(M), reject all compromises with the Congress, which they regard as the representative of the bourgeoisie and the main enemy of the people, consider the USSR as revisionist, and envisage the establishment of a people's democratic state led by the workers and the peasants with the national bourgeoisie as an ally. While they participate in parliamentary elections, they leave the possibility of armed struggle open if all the avenues for a peaceful transition are closed. In general, the CPI has received support from the urban intellectuals and trade unions while the CPI(M) has attracted the peasant cadres and has established its strongest bases among the peasants of the countryside. In Kerala, caste has also been detectable in the split; with some notable exceptions, the CPI has received support from higher castes, such as the Nairs, and the CPI(M) from the Harijans and the Ezhavas. Ever since the split, Kerala has been one of the two major strongholds of the CPI(M) (the other one being West Bengal), and within Kerala, Alleppey district has been one of its most important bases. But even in Alleppey district both the higher leadership of the old undivided Party and the urban-based trade unions, including the Coir Factory Workers' Union, have supported the CPI. On the other hand, the local leaders of the Thiruvitamkoor [Travancore] Karshaka Thozhilali Union, together with the vast majority of its rank and file members, cast their lots with the CPI(M). It is noteworthy that the TKTU lost its Alleppey-based leaders to the CPI. Among them were Varghese Vaidyan and S. K. Das, the president and secretary of the union, respectively, and its first two organizers. By the time the split occurred in 1964 the union had an office building in Alleppey which served as its state headquarters. Initially, there was some dispute as to which faction had the claim on this building. But in a meeting convened to discuss this question the CPI leaders are reported to have walked out when it became clear that they had little support within the union. It is reported that out of the thirty-three members in the managing committee less than half a dozen supported the CPI.

While the split in the Communist Party had many causes, there is little doubt that events in Kuttanad also represented an indictment of the higher-level leaders of the movement. It is important to note that these men were generally urban-based, higher caste, relatively wealthier, and more educated, while the vast majority of the membership as well as the local-level leaders were lower caste, less educated, and agricultural labourers or from agricultural labour background. It is possible that the split reflected a conflict of interest between higher and local-level leaders whose aspirations for mobility were thwarted by the former. On the other hand, it also seems possible that the higher leadership was gradually becoming elitist, reformist, revisionist, and generally unresponsive to the aspirations of the masses which had already been aroused. Some informants report that during the CPI's term of office between 1957 and 1959 these leaders were becoming more and more alienated from the masses and showing their unwillingness to lead struggles in the fields.[13] Later developments seem to suggest that these accusations are not altogether without foundation. The agricultural labour union led by the CPI today leads very few struggles in Kuttanad and is very much alienated from the masses of the workers.

Ever since the split in the CPI in 1964 the centre of the trade union scene in Kuttanad has been occupied by the union led by the CPI(M). But it was organized on a state-wide basis only in 1968, and its first state convention was held in 1970. At the state level it is known as the *Kerala State Karshaka Thozhilali* (Agricultural Labour) *Union* (KSKTU) and is affiliated to the CPI(M)-led trade union movement at the national level, the Centre of Indian Trade Unions (CITU). In 1975 it had a membership of 43,000 in Alleppey district and 159,000 in the state. In the district the strength of its membership is more than four times that of the next biggest union led by the CPI. It may also be noted that Alleppey district accounts for 27 per cent of its total membership in the state. In 1971-72 the percentage was 35—an indication of its growing strength in other districts of the state and perhaps also of its relatively declining rate of growth in Alleppey district itself.

The agricultural labour front of the CPI, however, was in disarray for at least two years after the split in the party. This organization, known as the *Kerala State Karshaka Thozhilali Federation* (KSKTF), became active only in 1970. The union is affiliated to the Kerala State Trade Union Council and to the All India Trade Union Congress (AITUC), the party's trade union front. It is important to note that by this time the CPI had become the major ruling party in Kerala and continued in power to the time of this study. The party has clearly taken a reformist view toward its union activities. It sees the union as an instrument in mobilizing support for the party and in putting pressure on the government to introduce and implement legislation for the betterment of the workers. It has little militancy, arouses little enthusiasm among the workers, and rarely leads struggles in Kuttanad. In fact, it is little more than a bureaucratically organized pressure group. Its leaders speak eloquently of the great achievements and struggles of the agricultural labour movement prior to 1964, but have little to say about its present activities or plans. They blame the workers for their failure. They bitterly complain about the workers' lack of seriousness and revolutionary consciousness, their emotionalism, and their eagerness to shout slogans, their gullibility. They say that when meetings are arranged the workers are eager to have the loudspeakers turned towards the direction of a hated landlord's house. They speak of the excesses in the past. It is clear that their view of the agricultural labour union and of its role have changed considerably since the early years of the movement. They have become clearly elitist and seem to be afraid of the risks in mobilizing the masses of the workers who, they think, need a good deal more education and guidance.

It seems certain that the split in the CPI had the effect of slowing down the momentum of the agricultural labour movement in Kuttanad. Although Kuttanad emerged as one of the strongest bases of the newly formed CPI(M) in Kerala and the agricultural labour union there became a staunch front of the party, the latter did not regain its active and militant character until 1967, when a CPI(M)-led united front government came to power in Kerala. From 1967, however, the union-led agitations and struggles increased in number and intensity. The agrarian scene began to be quiet again only when the CPI(M) entered its new phase of collaborating with the Kerala Congress in 1973-74. Oommen has collected cases relating to agrarian agitation in Alleppey district from 1965 to 1967. These are reproduced in Table 19. Between 1959 and 1967 Kerala had been under the rule first of the Praja Socialist Party and the Congress Party and then of the Indian president for a period of two years. It seems evident from the table that 1967 marked a resurgence of militant activities by the union.

TABLE 19: CASES RELATING TO AGRARIAN AGITATION IN ALLEPPEY DISTRICT FROM 1 JANUARY 1965 to 31 DECEMBER 1969

Party in Power and Period of Rule	No. of Cases Registered by Police and Charged to Courts	No. of Persons Arrested	No. Hurt	Violence of other Types
President's Rule 1 January 1965 to 31 December 1966	6(3)	132(66)	0	6(3)
United Front with CPI(M) as the Major Partner. 1 January 1967 to 31 December 1969	96(32)	477(159)	51(17)	44(15)

Note: Annual averages are shown in brackets.
Source: T. K. Oommen, *Agrarian Tension in a Kerala District: An Analysis* (New Delhi: Sri Ram Centre for Industrial Relations), p. 255.

Among the demands put forward by the union at this time there were two which led to some violent struggles. One related to the question of who had the right to be employed by a landlord. Anxious to maintain at least some control over their workers, many landlords began selecting their workers carefully, replacing the ''troublesome'' (which usually meant KSKTU-affiliated) workers with loyal ones. To counter this the Marxist-led union pressed for the recognition of the right of the *parisarathozhilalikal,* or workers living in the vicinity of a field, to be employed in that field. This was a radical demand in that it questioned the right of the landowners to employ the workers of their choice; it also sought to establish the workers' right to be employed. The second demand related to the choice of the field in which threshing was to be carried out. Traditionally, the labourers were required to carry the harvested sheaves to the threshing fields near the landlord's residence. Now the workers demanded that threshing must also be done in the same field in which the paddy was harvested.

An important struggle involving these two demands took place in 1968 in the field of an avowed and veteran anti-communist leader, E. John Jacob, who was also a member of the state legislative assembly and one of the most important state leaders of the Kerala Congress. Jacob answered the workers' demands by saying that he was master of his own house, that he would employ whom he chose and would have his threshing floor where he pleased. The labourers threatened to harvest his field by force. Both sides prepared for a confrontation, gathering about 5,000 people on each side. The workers were led by one of the senior local leaders, who was joint secretary of the KSKTU and member of the Alleppey district secretariat of the CPI(M). As violence broke out, the police interfered, resorted to *lathi* charge (clubbing) and eventually shooting, killing one worker. Many workers, including the leader, were manhandled and beaten up.[14] Two years later in 1970 there was another confrontation of a similar kind involving the same two issues in the field of a wealthy landlord. Here, too, events took a violent turn, resulting in police firing and in the death of a worker.

In January 1970 a state-wide land grab movement was launched under the leadership of the Marxist-led agricultural labour union. Although different phases of this campaign have continued to be organized periodically since then, its most violent and extensive phase seems to have taken place in 1970. On 31 October 1969 the CPI(M)-led government of E. M. S. Namboothiripad fell and was replaced by a mini-front government headed by the CPI. The new government prepared to implement the Land Reforms (Amendment) Act of 1969, which would come into effect on 1 January 1970. As noted before, two of the most important provisions of the act affecting agricultural labourers were those for conferring ownership rights to kudikidappukars and for taking over and redistributing excess land. The government prepared to implement these through the existing bureaucratic machinery. The kudikidappukars were required to submit applications to the revenue department requesting the transfer of title deeds. The act also required them to pay 12.5 per cent of the market value of the land in twelve instalments.

The developments leading to the formation of the new government had led to bitter hostility between the two Communist parties. It is believed by many people that the CPI(M) was determined to make the smooth functioning of the new government difficult. On the other hand, the leaders of the CPI(M) and the KSKTU argue that the government was not serious about implementing the land reform provisions quickly, but was capitulating to landlord interests. If the workers did not seize their land now, there was a danger that the machinations of the landlords, supported by the bureaucrats and the government, would dispose of the lands once and for all. In any case, a joint convention of the CPI(M)-led labour union and the farmer's union took the following decisions: 1) kudikidappukars must refuse to pay any rent for 10 cents (.04 ha) of land surrounding their houses; 2) they must fence the 10 cents of land around their homesteads and take yields from them; 3) groups of volunteers must occupy excess land by force; 4) preparations should be made to resist attempts by landlords or the police to prevent the execution of these decisions. The agitation began on 1 January 1970. Thousands of kudikidappukars asserted their ownership rights to 10 cents each of kudikidappu land by putting up fences around them and taking coconuts and other crops. Out of the estimated 70,000 hutment dwellers in Alleppey district, 20,000 are reported to have participated in this movement. It led to many violent confrontations, and at least two workers were killed in Kuttanad. According to Oommen, 10,000 cases relating to the land grab agitation were registered in the 11 civil and criminal courts in the district between 1 January and 31 May 1970 involving an estimated 25,000 accused.[15] As for occupying excess lands, there were a total of 931 encroachments and 338 houses were reported to have been built by the encroachers. The total number arrested were 4,881 amongst whom 4,489 were agricultural labourers and 32 were landowners. With the exception of two workers who belonged to the Praja Socialist Party, all the workers were affiliated to the CPI(M).[16]

It was clear that the campaign to take over the homesteads of the kudikidappukars evoked the most enthusiastic support and received the widest participation on the part of the landless labourers. It centred upon an elemental demand of the landless labourers, one on which their hopes had been raised at least since 1957. And, more importantly, it promised immediate and tangible results which appeared quite practical and within reach. By contrast, the campaign to occupy excess land had a more remote and symbolic aim. Although the campaign rhetoric included threats of occupying the excess lands until the government took them over and redistributed them to the landless, it was clear that its organizers had neither the resources nor the will to do so. In fact, the leaders of the campaign agreed that it had a more modest aim: to identify all the excess lands and to make their existence a matter of public knowledge. This, they hoped, would put pressure on the government to take them over and distribute them to the landless.[17] As shall be seen later, the campaign has continued to be organized year after year, evoking less and less enthusiasm on the part of the agricultural labourers.

THE KUTTANAD INDUSTRIAL RELATIONS COMMITTEE AND THE DEVELOPMENT OF
COLLECTIVE BARGAINING

Some of the ways in which the Kuttanad IRC has attempted to settle disputes
between farmers and agricultural labourers have already been described. Established under the initiative of the first Communist government in Kerala in 1957,
it is a tripartite body consisting of representatives from the government, the
farmer-employers, and the agricultural labourers. The last two are elected by the
organizations of the respective groups, and their numbers have varied from eight
to nine each. Since 1957 most of the important issues relating to farmer-labour
relations in Kuttanad have come before the IRC, which has made many decisions
regarding these. A few meetings of the body have been personally convened by
the chief minister or the labour minister of Kerala.

The rationale behind the IRC seems to be to institutionalize a process of collective bargaining, gradually eliminating the class hostility and confrontation that
has existed in Kuttanad during the past three decades. According to a decision
taken by the IRC on 19 October 1965, the unions are required to put before the
IRC all their new demands before the commencement of the crop season every
year. Only in the event of the failure of the IRC to arrive at a settlement satisfactory to them may they resort to other methods to meet their demands. Another
decision of the body taken in the presence of the labour minister in 1971 stipu-
lates that there should be yearly wage revisions tied to the changes in the consumer price index. These decisions have not been implemented as yet, but if they
are put into effect seriously, they are likely to change the situation in Kuttanad
quite radically.

It is not necessary to analyse here all the decisions made by the IRC. All parties agree that the IRC has helped to reduce the extent of conflict in Kuttanad by
providing a forum for collective bargaining and discussion. However, there are
many factors that limit the effectiveness of this body as an instrument for the resolution of conflict. One of these is the existence of rival organizations, especially
among the agricultural labourers. It appears that all the unions are given equal representation regardless of the strength of their membership. The KSKTU
workers complain that they have been unfairly treated by the CPI government
which manipulates different unions under the control of different political parties
and denies their union a voice in proportion to its membership. In any case, they
seem to believe strongly that they can win their rights only through struggle, for
which their numerical strength is an asset, and that the IRC can, at best, only
sanction or legitimize their successes won through struggle.

It is not surprising, therefore, that the CPI(M)-led KSKTU relies on its own
resources, especially on its ability to organize mass struggles. Often it presses its
demands through strikes and other similar methods without waiting for an IRC
decision. Sometimes it refuses to abide by an IRC decision to which it did not
consent. In actual fact, it is able to exercise a kind of veto power since no deci-

sion can be actually implemented without its consent. An instance of this kind arose in 1973-74 when the IRC met to settle new wage rates for the year. It fixed a wage rate of Rs. 9 for a male worker and Rs. 6-50 for a female worker. The KSKTU delegates rejected the decision. KSKTU-led workers began demanding Rs. 10 and 7 respectively from the employers. Many farmers began paying them this amount even without a struggle. As these rates became established facts, both the AITUC (CPI union) and the INTUC (Congress-led union) made statements supporting the KSKTU demand. The KSKTU workers maintain that the earlier decision of the IRC was made without consulting their representatives. The government, they say, had arrived at a prior settlement with the other trade unions (all of which are led by parties in the ruling united front). It appears that their action was not so much a struggle for the slight increase in wage as an assertion of their position *vis-à-vis* the other unions. Apart from all this, however, there is a more basic reason for the attitude of the KSKTU towards the IRC—a theme which will be discussed more fully in the next chapter. There is a basic ambiguity in the position of the CPI(M) towards institutions of this kind. The fulfilment of the aims of the IRC is likely to mean the failure of the cause of the CPI(M)—the promotion of class struggle and revolution.

THE 1970's—A CHANGE IN THE PATTERN?

Since the early 1970's some changes have become noticeable on the agrarian front in Kuttanad. After the land grab movement of 1970-71, when political militancy and violence reached a peak, the situation seems to have become calm and peaceful. By 1974-75 conflicts and confrontations had all but disappeared from the agrarian scene in Kuttanad. Although it was difficult to interpret the significance of what was happening, it seemed clear that the CPI(M)-led labour movement showed less militancy and enthusiasm than in the past. There was a widespread feeling in all circles that it may have entered a period of decline. There was also a widely held belief [acknowledged even by the CPI(M)][18] that rival trade unions, especially the ones led by the Congress and the RSP, may have been making some inroads into traditional KSKTU territories in some parts of Kuttanad.

One of the most important factors in this seems to have been the changed political situation and the changes in political alignments in Kerala, the impact of which was nowhere as significant as in Kuttanad. It has been mentioned before that following the fall of the CPI(M)-led government in 1969, a united front government headed by the CPI has exercised power in Kerala until now (1975). The requirements of realpolitik brought the CPI(M) and the Kerala Congress together into the opposition.[19] Negotiations for an electoral alliance were about to be finalized when the Indian government proclaimed a state of internal emergency, effectively suspending all political activities of opposition parties and indefinitely postponing the long-awaited elections in Kerala. Although the new strategy led to some confusion in the minds of the rank and file in both parties and even forced a split in the Kerala Congress, it considerably reduced the antagonism between the two organizations of class enemies in Kuttanad. To be sure, this required ideological reinterpretation of their positions by both the parties, sometimes directly contradicting their previous positions. In speeches and pamphlets the message was heard on all sides that the farmer and the labourer were on two sides of the same coin, not enemies but colleagues who ought to stand together united both to fight their common enemies and to increase production. For the first time in more than a decade, two years, 1974 and 1975, passed by without any new demands being made by the KSKTU.

As has been seen above, the existence of the IRC and the development of collective bargaining have also helped to reduce conflicts. At any rate, during the past few years all parties are showing greater willingness to make accommodations and compromises that are believed to be helpful to avoid needless confrontations and violence. Even the police have become much more cautious than in the past. At this point it is useful to describe the way in which various parties arrive at such accommodation in a typical situation.

One of the most difficult issues in Kuttanad for some years has been that of controlling the number of workers for harvesting. The IRC decided that the number should be restricted to 125 per hectare. Even after this decision, however, harvesting in the larger fields continued to be accompanied by violence and to require police protection. But today the situation is changing. A typical harvesting operation proceeds as follows. The landowner is required by law to obtain permission from the revenue office before harvesting. He announces the date of his harvest and requests police protection in advance. In addition, he approaches the local KSKTU leader or leaders and reaches prior understanding that no trouble will be caused. He would very likely have made a "contribution" to the labour union. The morning of the harvest arrives with the police on the scene and about 2,000 workers instead of the 250 that are supposed to be accommodated. When the first 225 have been let into the field, respecting the rights of workers of the vicinity, the landlord, the police officer, and the local union leader hold a brief discussion. The union leader suggests that another 400 workers could be accommodated. The police officer then says to the landlord, "Sir, don't you think we could allow another 200 into the field?" Almost certainly, the landlord accepts the suggestion. The officer then asks the remaining crowd to look for work elsewhere. In fact, many will already have left for another harvest site.

It is now widely believed that the CPI(M) leadership, long thought to be incorruptible, has begun to be corrupt like other politicians. Some are said to receive regular bribes from larger farmers anxious to avoid trouble in their fields, but it seems that although corruption is on the increase in the KSKTU and the CPI(M), these are still the least corrupt political organizations in the area. [I know with certainty of only one CPI(M) leader who had accepted bribes from farmers.] Nevertheless, it seems certain that there is a measure of disenchantment among the rank-and-file workers who are no longer as willing to confront the police or the landlords' thugs as they once were in the recent past; it is becoming more difficult to assemble large crowds for a demonstration or a struggle. In March 1975 two Marxist party workers were murdered and a third seriously injured by a Congress-affiliated landlord and his hirelings. One of the murdered party workers was a leader of some importance. The party called a one-day strike throughout Alleppey district and organized an impressive funeral procession in which tens of thousands took part. Some state leaders of the party later visited the homes of those killed and conveyed their condolences to the bereaved members of their families. The matter seemed to end there, and the situation in Kuttanad soon became normal again. Informed people in Kuttanad say that only two or three years ago an incident of this kind would have almost certainly sparked off a wave of violent protests all over Kuttanad.

Only one major struggle organized by the KSKTU took place during field work for this study in Kuttanad between September 1974 and September 1975. At a special convention in Quilon in February 1975 the KSKTU state leadership gave the call to begin the sixth phase of its state-wide campaign to occupy excess land still in the hands of landowners. After long preparations and planning the campaign began on 17 April with great fanfare and publicity. The state secretary of the KSKTU launched the campaign by leading a group of volunteers onto excess land belonging to the former Maharaja of Travancore in Trivandrum. The party's daily, *Deshabhimani,* and the union's monthly *Karshaka Thozhilali,* reported in detail the progress of the campaign in each district. The other newspapers in the state largely ignored it after the first day's events. In each of the localities where a struggle took place a group of volunteers entered a plot of land that had already been marked as excess, "occupied" the land by planting a red flag, at times planting some new crop, or taking crops from the land. Defence committees were reportedly organized to defend the occupied land against attacks from the landlord, his agents, or the police.

The campaign ended, at least temporarily, on 1 May, International Labour day. The secretary of the Alleppey district unit of the KSKTU summed up the results of the campaign in the district: roughly 10,000 volunteers had entered 16,800 hectares of excess land in 61 centres in the district. Police had registered cases against 1,500 men and had arrested 185 and detained them for short periods. To protect the occupied land, "excess land defence committees had already begun to take the necessary steps."[20]

Throughout the campaign I had made persistent efforts to accompany a group of volunteers, or at least to be personally present at the site of a struggle. It was a difficult task, as the locations of the actual struggles were a strictly kept secret in order to keep the police away. The higher leaders, who were generally more willing to co-operate, did not themselves know the actual sites of the struggles. Upon making long trips to the places they suggested, I found that the local leaders had altered their previous plans, either changing the date or the site of the struggle. Eventually I succeeded in arriving at the site of an actual struggle, in the village of Kumarankari, and was taken by a guide to a small and isolated house in which about eight or nine men were having a tea party. The guide introduced me to the ward president who was supposed to have been the leader of the party. When asked when they were going to begin the "struggle," someone replied, "We started about two hours ago. It is over for today." They showed me a red flag planted in the middle of an otherwise deserted field. I complained to a senior taluk-level leader that I was missing all these events because no one was giving me the correct information. He said I had not missed much; there was not very much to see. They had simply planted a red flag, and then he had given a short speech. That was all.

It was evident that the campaign represented anything but a mass upsurge. It was organized from the top, and the groups of volunteers who occupied the excess lands were mostly party or union functionaries. There was no enthusiasm among the masses. For the most part, the campaign was ignored by the workers, the press, and even the landlords and police.[21] To be sure, whenever the police were given information about illegal entry into land and the plucking of coconuts and other crops, those involved had to be charged, and some were even taken into custody for brief periods. The campaign was, however, significant in one respect. Although few landlords in Kuttanad have excess land on paper, local labourers and union officials have fairly accurate knowledge of the extent of excess land held in their own areas. And, in general, the lands occupied during the campaign were in fact excess lands held illegally. After the occupation, the list of these lands is made public by the union and its organs. The campaign thus at once establishes the moral right of the workers to occupy lands which belong to them and puts pressure on the government and others concerned to implement the provisions of the land reforms. The excess land campaign has made it more difficult for them to claim, as some have attempted to do, that there is no excess land in the hands of landlords.[22]

6

Conclusion: Agrarian Class Conflict, Trade Unionism, and Democratic Politics

It was the intention of this study to examine the structural roots and dynamics of agrarian conflict in Kuttanad. The development of the productive forces in Kuttanad, the evolution of its agrarian relations, the emergence of a relatively large and impoverished rural proletariat and its political mobilization and struggle have been discussed in detail. It now remains to draw some general conclusions from this analysis, attempting to spell out more specifically the answers to some of the important questions raised in the first chapter.

CONDITIONS OF AGRARIAN CLASS MOBILIZATION AND STRUGGLE

It is generally recognized that causal explanations of social phenomena are difficult if not altogether impossible, and that even attempts to identify and describe the conditions under which social phenomena occur are fraught with pitfalls. This is so because social action, in our case political action of agrarian classes, does not lie entirely within the world of determinism. Yet, the most important contribution of sociology has been to show how social action is constrained, limited, and even spurred by concrete structural and historical conditions. Once the inherent limitations have been recognized, it is possible and necessary for the sociologist to identify and describe, at least in broad terms, some of the most important of these conditions. Of course, the conditions or factors that influence a particular social phenomenon are numerous. Those that have influenced the development of class struggle in Kuttanad range from ecological conditions to the strategies and tactics of the Communists in India. Most of these have been described in Chapters 2 through 5. What follows here are some brief comments on five general categories or sets of factors which subsume all the others.

The first and the most obvious of these concerns the concrete development of class relations in the area. It is obvious that an agricultural labour movement cannot arise without there being an agricultural labour class, just as a proletarian revolution cannot occur without a significant urban proletariat. Among the types of circumstances specified by scholars as being associated with high levels of agrarian conflict in India in recent decades two are particularly noteworthy: a sharp polarization of the agrarian structure, and a high proportion of agricultural labourers.[1] Kuttanad is outstanding in both these respects. In Kuttanad the agricultural labourers constitute a class, a rural proletariat, both in the sense of a class "in itself" and to a large extent also a class "for itself." As has been noted before, in areas where the basic polarization is between landlords and tenants rather than between farmers and landless labourers (or is at least perceived as being so by leaders and organizers) the agrarian movement is led by the tenants, who are generally rich and middle peasants. The agricultural labourers are likely to remain on the sidelines of the political process.

Scholars who have investigated the major peasant revolutions of the twentieth century have generally ascribed a crucial role in these revolutions to the middle peasant.[2] Many students of Indian society, on the other hand, have found that the agricultural labourers and poor peasants show the greatest militancy and potential for radical political action.[3] This study may provide an explanation for this divergence. It has shown that in Kuttanad the middle peasant, that is, the independent small holder, is practically a non-existent class. Even relatively small peasants who employ agricultural labour and do not work as wage labourers themselves tend to be conservative and to support the large landowners. Furthermore, it should be noted that such writers as Wolf and Alavi discuss the relative importance of agrarian classes (not only their political orientations but also their tactical power) in the context of actual revolutions and armed uprisings, mostly successful, while the others attempt to assess the revolutionary potential of these classes on the basis of their participation in trade union activities and parliamentary politics and in isolated abortive and short-lived armed uprisings. It may very well be that in the event of armed struggle, the agricultural labourers of Kuttanad, too, will find that by themselves they possess little tactical power for the struggle.

Another set of factors is the material preconditions that make possible both the development of class consciousness and the organization of that consciousness for political purposes. The well-known Marxist position in this regard is that for these developments to take place certain minimum material and technical conditions must be present. These are necessary in order to break down the isolation of the village community or the parish, to establish mutual multiple relationships among men across these boundaries, and to create an awareness of their commonality of situation and of interests. Typically, this task is accomplished by an expanding capitalist economy and the many developments that accompany it, such as the modern factory that brings large numbers of men together or modern transportation and communication facilities. While it is largely true that "class consciousness is a phenomenon of the modern industrial era,"[4] this era is also one of world capitalism and imperialism, and today such conditions are present in many peasant and agrarian societies, as the peasant revolutions of this century amply illustrate. Some of the material and technical conditions present in Kuttanad have been described in Chapter 1. Without repeating all of these here, the following factors should be emphasized: Kuttanad's capitalist agriculture and factory-like paddy fields, in which literally thousands of men work together; its proximity to Alleppey; its relatively advanced transportation and communication systems and its openness to the outside world; and finally its high literacy, which makes the printed media a great instrument of mobilization. A caveat to be added here is that Kuttanad may not be a sufficiently large unit for the study of the kind of class consciousness that is typical of the modern era. Many locally based movements like that of Kuttanad must be integrated into larger and nationwide movements the conditions for which cannot be discussed here.

The third condition concerns the dissatisfaction arising from the rapid rate of social change that has been occurring in the region. Eric Wolf has argued that an essential initial condition for the successful mobilization of any peasant class is some disruption in traditional social arrangements. He adds that there are few processes that cause greater disruption to the pattern of peasants' life than the penetration of capitalism and market relations.[5] In Kuttanad, the substitution of cash payments for payments in kind and the withdrawal of traditional gifts by the farmers were simply part of the process of rationalization of production and the modernization of agriculture. They were also part of the process of proletarianization. It is interesting that many demands of the agricultural labourers have centred on the restoration or continued observance of customary payments and obligations. Rapid social change affects different social classes differentially, and the class or classes adversely affected are likely to experience relative deprivation, that is, deprivation either in relation to the position of other classes or to their own positions in the past. There seems little doubt that in Kuttanad tenancy reforms have aggravated the agricultural labourers' sense of relative deprivation. Referring to the land grab movement, a local labour leader commented:

> the landowners talk about the "injustice" being done by the labourers in grabbing their property. But only yesterday these lands were someone else's property. These landowners were tenants then. How did they become owners today? And they have no doubts about the "justice" in their grabbing these lands. Only when the agricultural labourer demands even a small portion of the land they shout "injustice."

Next, it is necessary to consider the role of primordial institutions which mediate the political mobilization of peasant classes and the development of their class consciousness, with specific focus on caste and caste ideology.[6] It is commonplace to argue that caste loyalties and caste ideology prevent the development of class consciousness.[7] I would suggest, on the contrary, that under certain circumstances caste may help to promote class consciousness by providing a certain amount of cultural homogeneity and already available sense of group identity and loyalty.[8] It is, however, true that the agricultural labour union today cuts across many castes, including even higher castes, and that the consciousness embodied in the union transcends caste consciousness. Nevertheless, I would argue that classes as historical formations have emerged out of already existing social groups with their own group consciousness. To the extent that class relations underlie caste relations and agricultural labourers are made up of Harijans and low castes, such an already available sense of identity and loyalty has been helpful in the development of class consciousness. This was especially true in the initial stages of the movements. As for the hold of the system-maintaining caste ideology on the Harijans, it may be pointed out that the people at the bottom layers of Indian society have always been much less committed to this ideology than the upper strata. Throughout Indian history the Harijans have shown a readiness to accept heterodox religious and political world views, be it Buddhism, Islam, Christianity, or, lately, communism. In Kerala, communism has had the greatest success in replacing the ideology of the *status quo;* it has presented to the lower classes an explanation of their condition and pointed to the possibility of changing it. It is noteworthy that a large proportion of Kerala's Harijans had already been converted to Christianity prior to their conversion to communism.

The fifth and last condition for the mobilization of agricultural labourers in Kuttanad is, in my view, the most important one. It is the existence and the availability of a party with the appropriate ideology and strategy to organize the discontent of the labourers. Without such an agency it is unlikely that the first step in their organization would ever have been taken. Not only is it unlikely that the labourers ever would have by themselves got the idea of organizing, but even if they had, their total dependence on their traditional masters made them extremely vulnerable to repression and to all forms of retaliation. It is significant to note that in Kuttanad many labourers who actively participated in struggles outside their villages were terrified and unwilling to face their own masters in their own villages. In course of time, their own mutual support as embodied in their organization provided them the necessary strength. But in the initial stages support had to come from elsewhere. The labourers required legal, financial, and even physical protection. Nowhere in the Indian countryside could local bosses be expected to accept the loss of their control over their former servants meekly; their instinctive reaction would likely be to intimidate and bully the latter by harassing them in many ways. Even today the union in Kuttanad spends a good deal of money and effort for the defense of its members who have been involved in lawsuits either as a result of actual confrontations or of false charges made against them. The support of a well-established party and of a trade union was of immense help to the labourers. It may also be observed here that when men of high caste and class background were converted to the labourers' cause, it enhanced the prestige of the movement and provided great moral support to the labourers.

The importance of the party and of the workers' organization raises two further questions: the extent to which agricultural labourers have been inspired and led by outsiders; and the kind of alliances and linkages that have been established with other classes and groups. The view that the peasantry in general cannot secure its interests without outside leadership is an old one shared by Marxists and non-Marxists alike. Thus, in a discussion of the relationship between peasants and politics Hobsbawm maintains that "the idea of a general peasant movement, unless inspired from outside, or even better, from above, is quite unrealistic."[9] This has been generally borne out by scholars studying peasant movements and revolutions.[10] If this is true about peasants in general, it must be all the more true about agricultural labourers. There is little doubt that the achievements of the agricultural labourers of Kuttanad would not have been possible without the party. But the question is, in today's context, to what extent can the party be considered an outside phenomenon? Indeed, is there any movement or ideology that is purely indigenous to the Kerala village? To be sure, the Communist movement or the party is larger, stronger, and more resourceful than the agricultural labourers or than any of its constitutive parts; its ideology, in part even its leadership, have their origins outside Kerala. At the same time, however, it has deep roots in the soil of Kerala; it is the party of the agricultural labourers, the industrial workers, and various other classes of Kerala. Through its grass roots organization it has provided a mechanism for the agricultural labourers to represent themselves and their interests. Given the absence of any sharp rural-urban difference in Kerala, the conception of an "urban elite" organizing and leading the "rural peasantry" makes as little sense as that of a class of poor peasants rising in spontaneous revolt. The Communist leadership in Kerala (and to a lesser extent the political elite in general) have their roots in the villages and are not greatly separated from the ordinary villagers socially or culturally. Although the higher leadership tends to come from the upper castes and classes, it is remarkable that a large number of important leaders are, in fact, drawn from the lowest strata of society. It is significant that both the state president and secretary of the KSKTU have agricultural-labour as well as low-caste backgrounds, being a Harijan and an Ezhava respectively.

The party acts an an umbrella under which alliances and linkages with other classes and groups are established and maintained. The relationship between the agricultural labourers of Kuttanad and the coir factory workers of Alleppey is such a linkage. In fact, the agricultural labour union in Kerala as a whole has strong alliances with and receives support from many organizations and trade unions working under the auspices of the same parent party. The toddy-tappers' union has been of particular importance in this respect. These two unions provide the backbone of the CPI(M) in Kerala today. What has been much more problematic is the question of establishing links with other agrarian classes and their organizations. It is true that there is a farmers' organization working under the auspices of the CPI(M) and that it collaborates with the KSKTU, but this organization has little significance in Kuttanad or in Kerala. We have argued that in the Kerala context, the agricultural labourers can count as potential allies only those small peasants who engage in at least some wage labour. It may be recalled that in Malabar, where the peasant movement has been dominated by tenant cultivators, agricultural labour interests remained neglected much longer than in Kuttanad, despite the strong Marxist influence in the area for a long time.

ACHIEVEMENTS OF THE AGRICULTURAL LABOUR MOVEMENT

It is necessary to make a distinction between the movement's trade union goals and other, more directly political goals during its three and a half decades of struggle. As a trade union it has been relatively successful. Indeed, the daily money wage rate of an agricultural labourer in Kuttanad today (Rs. 10 for a male worker and Rs. 7 for a female worker) is the highest anywhere in the country. And Kuttanad is one of the few regions in which working hours are fixed (7 hours a day in the kayal areas and 6 hours a day in the punja fields) and other working conditions are regulated. Furthermore, Kuttanad's agricultural labourers have successfully resisted mechanization, abolished all forms of forced labour or work without remuneration, and are largely free from abuses, ill-treatment, and the arbitrary use of power by the landowners. They have even won some limited rights in land. It is true that during this period the thrust of social and economic development in the area, as elsewhere in the country, may have been to push their living standards further down. It seems certain, however, that without the union and the struggles and without the wage increases, the deterioration in their living standards would have been far greater. Their achievements appear the more remarkable when compared with the degrading conditions of their unorganized counterparts in other parts of the country.[11]

THE MAKING OF A RURAL PROLETARIAN CLASS

The greatest achievement of the agricultural labour movement, perhaps, has been something more intangible. The mobilization and organized struggles of the agricultural labourers have entailed the development of their class consciousness. Admittedly, the concept of class consciousness is a difficult one and an adequate analysis of it ought to distinguish the various levels and degrees at which it can and must be understood. Thus, it can be seen as ranging from a sense of the commonality of situation to an understanding of the social order that rejects its claim to legitimacy.[12] In the broadest sense, and taking the concept to mean the minimal referents of a sense of the commonality of situation and interests, it can be said that the existence of an organization that has mobilized the agricultural labourers and inspired mass participation both implies and manifests class consciousness. Further, it may be claimed that the union, the movement, embodies the consciousness of the rural proletarian class, and the growth of the movement is also indicative of the growth of class consciousness. Not long ago, the agricultural labourers of Kuttanad were unorganized, powerless and oppressed, and divided among themselves by caste and patron-client bondage. Today, they have not only organized strength but a sense of their strength and power. They have become transformed into an organized, militant, and struggling class "for itself." There is a saying attributed to Sartre that a class is not given but made; it may be added that a class is made through struggle, through the sharing of hardships, failures, and above all, of at least some successes. It may be argued further that the maintenance of this class is predicated on common effort and common interests embodied in its organization. To the extent that this is true, it can be presumed that the class will cease to exist when the common venture ceases to exist; that is, the labourers will cease to exist as a class the moment they cease to exist as an organized, acting, and struggling class. In other words, class consciousness cannot be taken for granted. The solidarity of the class will disintegrate without the continued involvement and participation of the union.

Today, the agricultural labour union in Kuttanad has begun to show signs of such disintegration. It now organizes few practical programmes in which the workers participate actively. It seems to have reached a dead end and to be in need of a new path. Under such conditions the organization can gradually degenerate into a self-serving bureaucracy which cannot then be said to embody the interests and consciousness of the agricultural labour class. The problem, of course, is a classic one. The conditions of the working class make them utterly powerless without a strong and efficient organization. On the other hand, such an organization tends to be centralized and to usurp power into the hands of the bureaucrats, in extreme cases becoming completely totalitarian.[13] The solution to the problem requires both the institutionalization of genuinely democratic and participatory methods and a working class that is conscious of its rights and prepared to safeguard those rights.

CLASS STRUGGLE, TRADE UNIONISM, AND DEMOCRATIC POLITICS

The agricultural labour movement has been at once a trade union and an organization designed to mobilize the masses of the labourers for the class struggle and the revolution. However, as has been discussed, it has been most successful as a trade union. It is, of course, difficult to separate the purely trade-union-type activities of the organization from the revolutionary aspects of its work; both are intertwined, and such trade union activities as the strike are an integral part of the revolutionary mobilization of the agricultural labour class. Nevertheless, it is possible to discern shifts in emphasis both in the activities of the union and in the approach of the Communist parties towards the mobilization of agricultural labour. At least since India's independence in 1947, the Communists have shown a basic ambivalence in their approach to trade union work and the revolutionary mobilization of workers.

This ambivalence is the result, in part, of a certain contradiction between trade unionism and revolutionary class struggle. Trade unions typically aim at improving the conditions of the workers' lives within the framework of capitalism, accepting and accommodating to the class rule of the bourgeoisie. They abide by the bourgeois "rules of the game." Revolutionary movements, by contrast, aim at the destruction of the system and reject its rules. "What is thus really at stake," writes Mészaros, quoting Marx, "is not the issue of how to obtain 'a better wage for the slave', nor indeed that of a change in the tone of voice—carefully fitted by 'human engineering'—which transmits the dictates of commodity production to the workers, but a *radical restructuring* of the established order of society."[14] The difference between the two is one between reform and revolution. The agricultural labour movement in Kuttanad has been caught in a dilemma between the requirements of trade unionism and class struggle. On the one hand, they must establish their credibility as serious trade unionists and bargainers by convincing everyone of their commitment to collective bargaining and of their willingness to abide by the agreements arrived at. On the other hand, for the Communist parties, and especially for the CPI(M) and the union under its sponsorship (the union leaders are without exception party activists), trade union activities are only instruments for the revolutionary mobilization of the workers. Theoretically, at least, the tasks of the CPI(M) on the trade union front are clearly laid out in its documents:

> while attaching vital importance to the defence of the daily interests of the working class—it measures its own success and the success of the working class movement by the level of revolutionary consciousness created during the course of these struggles.[15]

And further,

> A worker can be said to have developed socialist consciousness when he realizes that he is destined to be a wage slave so long as the present social

order lasts, that his struggle for emancipation is not only against a particular employer or set of employers but against the state of the capitalist class which he must replace by a state of his own. Unless, therefore, he realizes that his interests are in complete contradiction to the existing social order and that he must wage continuous political battle against the rule of the capitalist class, he cannot be considered to be really class conscious. . . . It is the task in the trade union front movement to lead workers from the elementary trade union movement consciousness to this higher consciousness.[16]

The ambivalence is aggravated by the shifting approaches and strategies of the Communists. At the time of India's independence in 1947 the CPI failed to come up with an adequate analysis of the situation in the country and to define clearly its strategy and tactics. Almost by default, and no doubt with some inspiration from Moscow, it soon became involved in parliamentary politics. As Kathleen Gough has written,

Their leaders are now innured to electoral manoeuvering, to the detriment of revolutionary work. Yet, large numbers of peasants and workers still owe allegiance to these parties, which did conduct militant struggles in the 1930s and late 1940s and at various times have made small gains on behalf of their followers through trade union activities. Clinging to the parliamentary path, the leadership of these parties currently puts a brake on revolutionary organization.[17]

In general, the tendency on the trade union front seems to have been to eschew what are perceived to be the distant and remote revolutionary goals in favour of immediate and tangible economic ones. We have seen that even in terms of these goals the CPI's responses to the needs of Kuttanad's workers have been disappointing. The CPI(M) has done much better and has built a strong base in the region. But its strategy, too, is limited and, in practise at least, scarcely extends beyond trade union goals. Once these goals have been even partially achieved, as has been the case in Kuttanad, this strategy reaches a dead end. The KSKTU leaders in Kuttanad privately agree that incessant demands for wage increases may have begun to backfire and that Kuttanad's problems cannot be solved through wage increases alone. They have little to offer the workers, however, except their rhetoric and a vague promise that if and when they are elected to power they will industrialize Kuttanad and create more jobs. I was amazed to hear local CPI(M) leaders talk eloquently about the great progress achieved in establishing capitalist relations in agriculture. Their vision, at least for the foreseeable future, goes only as far as an ideal farmer-labour relationship; it does not extend to the abolition of that relationship and to the restructuring of society.

It seems that the agricultural labour movement in Kuttanad has now been integrated into the existing system. The reduction in militant struggles, the increasing institutionalization of collective bargaining and parliamentary politics are all indicative of this. In this respect, the political scientists who proclaim the triumph of accommodative politics in India may well have a point. It has been seen how the requirements of electioneering and realpolitik have led the leadership of the CPI(M) to accommodate and even to collaborate with organizations and parties of class enemies. Indeed, it seems that the Communist leadership of both the parliamentary parties has acquired a certain stake in the maintenance of the system. Many have important positions as members of parliament, of the provincial legislative assembly, even as cabinet ministers, which are relatively secure as long as they work within the system and retain their electoral support, although they are susceptible to pressure from more radical and militant cadres within the party.[18]

Despite all the shortcomings of the movement, it remains true that it is still the movement of the workers of Kuttanad. Indeed, it is the only organization that represents their interests and conducts struggles on their behalf. It is through this organization that they acquired an awareness of their rights as workers and as human beings, found self-respect and a sense of dignity, and gained their collective identity and organized strength. The future will depend on a variety of factors, most importantly perhaps on what happens to their sponsoring party or parties.[19] The irony is that many if not most of the determining factors may lie outside Kuttanad and even Kerala and may be beyond the control of its agricultural labourers. Nonetheless, the agricultural labourers have been able to maintain a degree of revolutionary consciousness, and the revolutionary potential in Kuttanad remains high.

Notes

NOTES TO CHAPTER ONE

1. Two outstanding examples are Barrington Moore, Jr., *Social Origins of Dictatorship and Democracy: Lord and Peasant in the Making of the Modern World* (Boston: Beacon Press, 1966) and more recently, Eric Wolf, *Peasant Wars of the Twentieth Century* (London: Faber and Faber, 1969).

2. Historians and economists seem to have devoted much greater attention to the peasantry, at least of Europe. See Teodor Shanin, *Peasants and Peasant Societies* (Harmondsworth: Penguin, 1971).

3. Of course, there has been a long Marxist tradition of scholarship and debate on these issues, but it has largely remained outside academic sociology. See, for example, Lenin's *The Development of Capitalism in Russia*, the earliest and one of the most brilliant of Lenin's works. *Collected Works*, vol. 3 (Moscow: Foreign Language Publishing House, 1960).

4. For instance, the work of Dharma Kumar has shown that pre-British society in south India contained a significant number of agrestic slaves. See Dharma Kumar, *Land and Caste in South India* (Cambridge: Cambridge University Press, 1965).

5. The "village community" in India has been the subject of a great deal of discussion among earlier writers on India, and this has proved to be a source of many errors in our understanding of Indian society. The picture given was that of a utopian "village republic," self-sufficient and unaffected by outside authority. So prevalent was this myth that Marx and later even Gandhi accepted it. A review of the development of ideas on the village community can be found in Louis Dumond, "The Village Community: From Munro to Maine," *Contributions to Indian Sociology*, December 1966. M. N. Srinivas and S. M. Shah have argued that the self-sufficiency of the Indian village is a myth fabricated by early British writers such as Sir Henry Maine. See their "The Myth of the Self-Sufficiency of the Indian Village," *Economic and Political Weekly* (Bombay), 1960 Special Number. There seems little doubt, however, that the pre-British Indian village enjoyed a certain measure of economic and political autonomy and remained in relative isolation.

6. For discussions of the nature of this relationship, see Andre Gunder Frank, *Capitalism and Underdevelopment in Latin America* (New York and London: Monthly Review Press, 1967); Robert I. Rhodes, *Imperialism and Underdevelopment* (New York and London: Monthly Review Press, 1970); J. D. Cockroft, A. G. Frank, and D. L. Johnson, *Dependence and Underdevelopment* (New York: Anchor Books, 1972).

7. See Wolf, *Peasant Wars*, and also his "On Peasant Rebellions," *International Social Science Journal* 21 (1969); Hamza Alavi, "Peasants and Revolution," in Kathleen Gough and Hari P. Sharma, *Imperialism and Revolution in South Asia* (New York and London: Monthly Review Press, 1973), pp. 291-337; Kathleen Gough, "Peasant Resistance and Revolt in South India," *Pacific Affairs* 41, no. 4 (Winter 1968-69): 526-44.

8. Important exceptions to this are Joan Mencher, "Agricultural Labour Movements in Their Socio-Political and Ecological Context: Tamil Nadu and Kerala," in *Culture and Society*, ed. Balakrishna N. Nair, (Delhi: Thomson Press, 1975), and "Agricultural Labour Unions: Some Socio-Economic and Political Considerations," paper presented to the International Congress of Anthropological and Ethnological Societies, Chicago, August-September 1973; Sydney Mintz, "The Rural Proletariat and the Problem of Rural Proletarian Consciousness," *Journal of*

Peasant Studies 1, no. 1 (1973): 290 and his several other contributions, especially "Canamelar: The Contemporary Culture of a Rural Puerto Rican Proletariat" (Ph.D. diss., Columbia University, 1951); H. A. Landsberger, *Rural Protest, Peasant Movements and Social Change* (London: Macmillan, 1973); Y. G. Alexandrov, "Peasants, Development and Nationalism," in ibid., and Andre Beteille, *Studies in Agrarian Social Structure* (Oxford: Oxford University Press, 1974).

9. Alexandrov, "Peasants, Development, and Nationalism," and Rodolfo Stavenhagen, *Social Classes in Agrarian Societies* (New York: Doubleday Anchor, 1975).

10. Census of India, 1971, Series I, Paper 1, Supplement, Provisional Population Totals, p. 30.

11. See, for instance, Hari P. Sharma, "The Green Revolution in India, Prelude to a Red One?" in Gough and Sharma, *Imperialism and Revolution*, and Francine Frankel, *India's Green Revolution: Economic Gains and Political Costs*, (Bombay: Oxford University Press, 1971), pp. 77-102.

12. Andre Beteille, "The Causes of Agrarian Unrest," in Beteille, *Studies in Agrarian Social Structure*, p. 189. It is true that agrarian conflicts have occurred also in many other parts of the country. In many well-known struggles (Tebhaga, Telengana, and more recently Andra and Bihar) tribal dispossession and/or unfavourable tenancies have been the major issues. The point to be noted here is that in many of the most recent struggles (Kerala, Tanjore, West Bengal) agricultural labourers have been emerging as a new force, and these have occurred mainly in the densely populated coastal areas of wet paddy cultivation.

13. The two available sociological studies on agrarian conflict in Kuttanad attribute too much importance to the Communists and imply that much of the conflict is caused by their activities. See T. K. Oommen, "Agrarian Tension in a Kerala District: An Analysis," Sri Ram Centre for Industrial Relations, Reprint Series no. 15 [New Delhi]; and K. C. Alexander, "Emerging Farm-Labour Relations in Kuttanad," *Economic and Political Weekly*, 25 August 1973.

14. Hamza Alavi, "Peasant Classes and Primordial Loyalties," *Journal of Peasant Studies* 1, no. 1 (1973): 23 ff.

15. *The Structure of Scientific Revolutions* (Chicago: University of Chicago Press, 1962).

16. Robert Redfield, *Tepoztlan, a Mexican Village: A Study of Folk Life*, (Chicago: University of Chicago Press, 1930). See also Andre Beteille, "Peasant Studies and Their Significance," in his *Six Essays in Comparative Sociology*, (Oxford: Oxford University Press, 1974), p. 21 ff.

17. Oscar Lewis, *Life in a Mexican Village: Tepoztlan Restudied* (Urbana: University of Illinois Press, 1951).

18. The important collection of essays edited by McKim Marriott, *Village India* (Chicago: University of Chicago Press, 1955). For studies on China inspired by this tradition see Fei Hsiao-Tung, *Peasant Life in China* (London: Routledge and Kegan Paul, 1939), Fei Hsiao-Tung and Chang Chin-I, *Earthbound China, A Study of Rural Economy in Yunnan* (London: Routledge and Kegan Paul, 1949).

19. Beteille, "Peasant Studies and their Significance," p. 21.

20. Among contemporary anthropologists who stress the uniqueness of the Indian system, the most prominent are L. Dumont, *Homo Hierarchicus* (London: Weidenfeld and Nicholson, 1970), and E. R. Leach, *Aspects of Caste in South India, Ceylon and North West Pakistan* (Cambridge: Cambridge University Press, 1960).

21. Beteille, "Ideas and Interests," in *Studies in Agrarian Social Structure*, p. 42.

22. Andre Beteille has compared this interpretation of Indian society to a similar interpretation by East European sociologists of their own societies. According to them there are no classes in their societies, but only 'strata'; if they are called classes at all, they are non-antagonistic classes. See Beteille, "Politics of Non-Antagonistic Strata," mimeographed, (Delhi School of Economics, 1969).

23. There is now much evidence to suggest that a good deal of mobility has always been possible within the caste system. See James Silverberg, ed., *Social Mobility in the Caste System in India, an Inter-Disciplinary Symposium* (The Hague: Mouton, 1968).

24. Gerhard Lenski, *Power and Privilege: A Theory of Social Stratification* (New York: McGraw Hill, 1966), pp. 5-17.

25. Stanislaw Ossowski, *Class Structure in the Social Consciousness* (New York: Free Press of Glencoe, 1963), ch. 4.

26. Gunnar Myrdal, *Asian Drama*, vol. 1 (New York: Pantheon 1968), p. 569.

27. See, for instance, Ralph Nicholas, "Structure and Politics in Villages of Southern Asia," in eds. M. Singer and B. Cohn, *Structure and Change in Indian Society* (New York and Chicago: Aldine Atherton, 1968); L. Rudolf and S. Rudolf, *The Modernity of Tradition* (Chicago: University of Chicago Press, 1967).

28. See my "Caste and Democracy in India" (M. A. thesis, Department of Sociology, York University, 1972).

29. Anthony Giddens, *The Class Structure of the Advanced Societies* (London: Hutchinson University Library, 1973), p. 19.

30. There are many reviews and analyses of the Marxist conception of class available in English. Some of the important ones are found in Ralf Dahrendorf, *Class and Class Conflict in Industrial Society* (Stanford: Stanford University Press, 1959), ch. 1; R. Bendix and S. M. Lipset, "Karl Marx's Theory of Social Classes," in Bendix and Lipset, *Class, Status and Power: Social Stratification in Comparative Perspective* (New York: Free Press, 1966),pp. 26-34; Giddens, *Class Structure of Advanced Societies*; and Stavenhagen, *Social Classes in Agrarian Societies*.

31. Lenin, "A Great Beginning," in *Selected Works*, vol. 2 (Moscow: Foreign Language Publishing House, 1952) p. 224.

32. See, for instance, Beteille, *Studies in Agrarian Social Structure*, especially "Ideas and Interests". For a discussion of the possibility of an objective determination of class interests, see Steven Lukas, *Power: A Radical View* (London: Macmillan, 1974).

33. One of the most notable examples is the case of China. It is, perhaps, noteworthy in this context that generations of anthropologists failed to foresee the upheavals now occurring in Africa.

34. V. I. Lenin, "What is to be Done?" in *Selected Works*, vol. 1 (Moscow: Progress Publishers, 1970); Antonio Gramsci, *The Modern Prince and Other Writings* (London: Lawrence and Wishart, 1957), pp. 172-73.

35. Istvan Mészaros, "Contingent and Necessary Class Consciousness," in I. Mészaros, ed., *Aspects of History and Class Consciousness* (London: Routledge and Kegan Paul, 1971), pp. 85-128.

36. Lenin's distinction between trade union consciousness and socialist consciousness is well known. Recently, Giddens has distinguished three levels of class consciousness. The first involves a conception of class identity (and therefore of class differentiation), the second a perception of conflict of interest, and the third, which alone is designated as revolutionary consciousness, involves "a recognition of the possibility of an overall reorganization in the institutional mediation of power . . . and a belief that such a reorganization can be brought about through class action," Giddens, *Class Structure of Advanced Societies*, pp. 112-13.

37. Marx, however, never lost interest in comparative and historical studies. His major ideas on precapitalist societies can be found in his *Pre-Capitalist Economic Formations*, ed. Eric Hobsbawm (New York: International Publishers, 1964).

38. Karl Marx, "The Eighteenth Brumaire of Louis Bonaparte," in *Selected Works*, vol. 1., pp. 478-79.

39. Alavi, "Peasant Classes and Primordial Loyalties," p. 26.

40. Lenin, *Development of Capitalism in Russia*. See also his *To the Rural Poor* in *Collected Works*, vol. 6. This book, written in 1903, attempts a breakdown of peasant classes in Russia. Out of a total of 10 million peasants in Russia there were 1.5 million rich peasants, 2 million middle peasants, and 6.5 million poor peasants. Lenin's ideas on peasant classes are also developed in his *Agrarian Question and the Critics of Marx*, in *Collected Works*, vol. 5.

41. Lenin, *Development of Capitalism in Russia*, p. 174.

42. Alavi, "Peasant Classes and Primordial Loyalties," p. 27.

43. Mao Tse-Tung, "How to Analyse the Classes in Rural Areas," *Selected Works*, vol. 1 (New York: International Publishers, 1954), pp. 138-40.

44. See *Central Committee Resolution on*

Certain Agrarian Issues and an Explanatory Note by P. Sundarayya, Communist Party of India (Marxist). The publication is undated, but this resolution was passed at the Central Committee meeting of the Party in Muzaffarpur in March, 1973. For an application of the model to the analysis of agrarian classes in Kerala see Indian School of Social Sciences, Trivandrum, "Agrarian Structure and Social Change in Selected Villages in Kerala: A Pilot Study of Three Villages", manuscript, 1973.

45. Alavi, "Peasants and Revolution," pp. 292-95.

46. Hamza Alavi, "India and the Colonial Mode of Production," *Economic and Political Weekly*, Special Number (August 1975). For further discussion on this and on the question of Kuttanad's class structure see Chapter 3.

47. Karl Polanyi has emphasized this point in his writings. See especially George Dalton, "Primitive, Archaic and Modern Economies: Karl Polanyi's Contribution to Economic Anthropology," *Proceedings of the 1965 Annual Spring Meeting of the American Ethnological Society*.

48. Quoted in Alavi, "Peasant Classes and Primordial Loyalties," p. 32.

49. See my "Caste and Democracy in India."

50. Quoted in Alavi, "Peasant Classes and Primordial Loyalties," p. 32.

51. Data on caste are not available in the Censuses taken after independence (1947). Collection of data on caste was dropped because the authorities felt that it encouraged "casteism," a phenomenon they viewed negatively.

52. For a discussion of some essential characteristics of working class organizations see Eric Hobsbawm, "Class Consciousness in History", in Istvan Mészaros, ed., *Aspects of History and Class Consciousness*, (London: Routledge and Kegan Paul, 1971), pp. 16-19.

NOTES TO CHAPTER TWO

1. Government of Kerala, *Report of the Kuttanad Inquiry Commission*, (Trivandrum, 1971), p. 4.

2. V. R. Pillai and P. G. K. Panikar, *Land Reclamation in Kerala* (New York: Asia Publishing House, 1965), p. 29.

3. *Report of Kuttanad Inquiry Commission*, p. 7.

4. Census of India, 1971, Series 9, Kerala, *District Census Handbook, Alleppey*, p. 45.

5. Government of Kerala, State Planning Board, *Economic Review Kerala, 1974* (Trivandrum, 1975), p. 36.

6. *District Census Handbook, Alleppey*, p. 45.

7. *Report of the Board of Conciliation of Trade Disputes in the Mats and Matting Industry 1939* (Trivandrum: Government Press, 1953), p. 70.

8. Ibid., p. 76.

9. National Council of Applied Economic Research, *The Techno-Economic Survey of Kerala* (New Delhi, 1962), p. 144.

10. Ibid., p. 300.

11. T. K. Oommen, "Agrarian Tension in a Kerala District: An Analysis," Sri Ram Centre for Industrial Relations, Reprint series no. 15, (New Delhi), p. 240.

12. Ibid., p. 41.

13. *Thiruvitamkoor Kayar Factory Workers' Union: Kanaka Jubilee Souvineer* [sic] (Quillon: Janayugam Press, 1972), Message by Revi Karunakaran, p. 6.

14. *Report of the Kuttanad Inquiry Commission*, p. 4.

15. *Kayal* is a Malayalam term which means a deep and extensive lake.

16. The Punja Special Officer, *A Note on Kuttanad and Punja Cultivation* (Trivandrum: Government Press, 1962), p. 2, and *Report of the Kuttanad Inquiry Commission*, p. 4.

17. Similar reclamations in the Netherlands, Japan, and the U.S.A. have been undertaken by the state, with the immense financial and technical resources at its command. See V. R. Pillai and P. G. K. Panikar, *Land Reclamation in Kerala* (New York: Asia Publishing House, 1965), p. 13.

18. *Report of the Kuttanad Inquiry Commission*, p. 5.

19. Ibid., and Pillai and Panikar, *Land Reclamation in Kerala*, pp. 14-15.

20. *Report of the Kuttanad Inquiry Commission*, p. 6.

21. This was shown in 1975 when the farmers

averted an economic disaster by constructing an emergency bund covering the unfinished portions of the Salt Water Barrier across the Vembanad lake at Thanneermukhom, about 24 kilometres north of the Kuttanad region. A relatively prolonged drought and the low water level in the rivers was leading to the intrusion of salt water into the lake, which was threatening to destroy an estimated 54,000 hectares of standing paddy worth Rs. 480 million. An emergency farmers' committee prepared and submitted to the government a proposal for the construction of a temporary bund at a cost of Rs. 500,000 while volunteers representing the farmers staged a 'sit in' in front of the district collector's office at Alleppey. The government's experts failed to come up with any feasible proposal even at a higher cost. With the government's approval and funds the farmers' committee supervised an emergency bunding project using the age-old techniques and 2,500 to 3,000 workers on a non-stop twenty-four hour basis. The work was completed in nineteen days before the salt water could do any damage to the crops.

22. It is believed by many people that such "sacrifices" and the "pouring of the blood" were commonly practised during the construction of railways and bridges in many places in and outside Kerala, especially by British engineers.

23. For earlier studies of the green revolution in India, see Francine R. Frankel, *India's Green Revolution: Economic Gains and Political Costs* (Bombay: Oxford University Press, 1971).

24. Government of Kerala, State Planning Board, Evaluation Division *Report on Intensive Agricultural District Programme in Kerala*, 1972, p. 6.

25. The data relating to new varieties, fertilizers, and so on, have been obtained from several people, among whom are the district agricultural officer and the Junior Research Officer at the Rice Research Station, Mankompu.

26. Government of Kerala, State Planning Board, Evaluation Division, *Report on Intensive Agricultural District Programme in Kerala*, 1972, p. 61.

27. Ibid., p. 104.

28. Oommen, "Agrarian Tension in a Kerala District," p. 235.

29. Government of Kerala, *Report on Intensive Agricultural District Programme*, p. 72

30. Ibid.

32. Computed from Ibid., p. 74.

32. Ibid., p. 72.

33. The *para* is a local measure. A standard para is 7.2 kg.

NOTES TO CHAPTER THREE

1. Joan Mencher, "Kerala and Madras: A Comparative Study of Ecology and Social Structure," *Ethnology* 5, no. 2 (1966): 135-71.

2. Ibid.

3. E. M. S. Namboothiripad, *The National Question in Kerala* (Delhi: People's Publishing House, 1952), chs. 2 and 3.

4. T. C. Varghese, *Agrarian Change and Economic Consequences: Land Tenures in Kerala, 1850-1960* (Bombay: Allied Publishers, 1970).

5. Ibid., p. 65.

6. Ibid.

7. In a strict sense, Syrian Christians are outside the framework of the Hindu caste system. However, traditionally they have functioned as a caste, accepting the caste rules, and have been so regarded by other castes. I shall therefore refer to them as a caste in this study. The Syrian Christians are an ancient Christian community whose history goes back to the very early centuries of the Christian era. The early Syrian Christians maintained close religious and trade relations with the Christians of the Middle East, and this is believed to explain their name as well as their use of Syriac and the Syrian rite. Today the majority of them are Roman Catholics (following the Syrian rite), some still belong to such ancient orthodox sects as the Jacobites, and others have embraced various protestant denominations.

8. Varghese, *Agrarian Change and Economic Consequences*, p. 112.

9. Ibid., p. 115.

10. Quoted in ibid., p. 114.

11. Ibid. See also V. R. Pillai and P. G. K. Panikar, *Land Reclamation in Kerala*

(New York: Asia Publishing House, 1965), ch. 6, for a detailed discussion of the financing of reclamation and farming in Kuttanad.

12. *Harijans* literally means "God's people," the name given by Gandhi to India's untouchable castes. They are also often referred to as scheduled castes because, together with the scheduled tribes, they come under the special provisions of the 6th schedule of the Indian constitution.

13. For a discussion of caste among the Christians of Kerala, see Ninan Koshy, *Caste in the Kerala Churches* (Bangalore, 1968).

14. An *illom* is the joint or extended patrilineal family of the Namboothiri Brahmins, the unit that owns land.

15. The Namboothiris of Kerala were left behind by the processes of modernization. For an account of their struggles to come to terms with modernity see the autobiography of E. M. S. Namboothiripad, *Athma Katha* (Trivandrum: Deshabhimani Book House, 1970).

16. The distinguished Indian historian, diplomat, and educator K. M. Panikkar, comes from such a family in Kuttanad. One of his ancestors, Eravi Kesava Panikkar, is generally agreed to have been the pioneer in kayal reclamation in Kuttanad. Another member of this family was the chairman of the municipal government of Alleppey at the time of this study.

17. The decline of the Nairs as a landed aristocracy has been one of the important aspects of social change in Travancore during the last hundred years. See Jeffrey Robin, *The Decline of Nayar Dominance: Society and Politics in Travancore 1847-1908* (New York: Holes and Meier, 1976).

18. *Census of Travancore*, 1931, Appendix IV, p. 472.

19. *Census of Travancore*, 1891, p. 470.

20. A valuable discussion of the social history of the Ezhavas can be found in A. Aiyappan, *Iravas and Culture Change* (Madras: Government Press, 1944).

21. Literally, "truth force," a form of struggle involving passive resistance made popular by Gandhi during the campaign for independence.

22. Computed from *District Census Handbook*, Alleppey, 1971.

23. Compiled from *District Census Handbook*, Alleppey, 1961, pp. 192-93.

24. Ibid.

25. For instance, Daniel and Alice Thorner, *Land and Labour in India* (Bombay: Asia Publishing House) ch. 3, Andre Beteille, *Studies in Agrarian Social Structure* (Oxford: Oxford University Press, 1974), especially chapters 1 and 3.

26. Pillai and Panikar, *Land Reclamation in Kerala*, p. 118.

27. K. Raman Unni, "Sources of Agricultural Labour in Kerala: Some Social Perspectives," in Balakrishna N. Nair, ed., *Culture and Society* (Delhi: Thomson Press, 1971).

28. Pillai and Panikar, *Land Reclamation in Kerala*, p. 49.

29. See K. C. Alexander, "Land Reform Legislations in Kerala Since Independence," *Behavioural Sciences and Community Development* 8, no. 2 (1974). See also the respective acts (Government Press, Trivandrum).

30. This government has achieved the distinction of having been the first and only one so far in Kerala to complete a full five-year term in office. In fact, thanks to the state of emergency in effect in India today, the government continued to hold power even after its term expired in 1975.

31. 1 cent = .01 acres = .004 hectares.

32. K. C. Alexander, "Land Reform Legislations in Kerala," p. 151.

33. It is possible that the land ceiling may have been much more effective in other areas of Kerala, especially in Malabar. Joan Mencher notes that in many parts of Palghat and Trichur Districts "it was rare to find a village household exceeding the ceiling" ("Limitations of Flexibility and their Implications for the Creation of a Socialist State: The Case of Kerala," paper presented at the American Anthropological Association annual meeting, Toronto, 1972).

34. It should be noted that we are here concerned with the classical middle peasant, the independent peasant cultivator whose class position is defined not simply by the amount of land owned, but by the independence, self-sufficiency, and tactical power that flow from his ownership of land as well as from his lack of dependence on hired labour.

There are no statistical data showing the exact extent to which small holders in Kuttanad use hired labour. Some available data for Kerala as a whole are reproduced below. It should be noted, however, that the small-holder in Kuttanad uses hired labour to a greater extent than the small holder in Kerala as a whole.

PERCENTAGE DISTRIBUTION OF HOLDINGS WITHIN EACH SIZE-CLASS ACCORDING TO THE NATURE OF LABOUR EMPLOYED: KERALA, 1970-71

Holding (ha)	Household members (%)	Household members and others (%)	Mostly wage-labour (%)
.04-.25	70.30	15.47	14.23
.25-.50	51.39	26.55	22.06
.50-1.0	37.97	32.09	29.94
1.0-2.0	28.09	33.18	38.73
2.0-4.0	19.36	33.49	47.15
4.0 & above	9.01	23.33	67.66

Source: *The Third Decennial World Agricultural Census, 1970-71 Report for the Kerala State*, Bureau of Economics and Statistics, Kerala.

35. Most of the contributions to the debate have appeared during the past ten years in the *Quarterly Review of Agriculture* of the *Economic and Political Weekly* and the *Social Scientist* published by the Indian School of Social Sciences in Trivandrum. For useful surveys of the debate see especially Hamza Alavi, "India and the Colonial Mode of Production," *Economic and Political Weekly*, Special Number (August 1975), and Doug McEachern, "The Mode of Production in Indian Agriculture," *Journal of Contemporary Asia* (1976): 444-57. For a similar and well-known debate on Latin America see Andre Gunder Frank, *Capitalism and Underdevelopment in Latin America* (New York: Monthly Review Press, 1967) and Ernesto Laclau, "Feudalism and Capitalism in Latin America," *New Left Review* (May-June 1971): 19-38.

36. See Gunder Frank, *Capitalism and Underdevelopment*, and Alavi, "India and the Colonial Mode of Production." Alavi's rationale for constructing this new concept is the importance he assigns to these unique features of a dependent economy.

37. Their situation may be compared to that of the poor whites in the United States. Like the poor whites who are apprehensive about the increasing power and freedom of the blacks, they feel more easily threatened by the growing power of the Harijan labourers and tend to identify with the wealthy and well-to-do farmers.

NOTES TO CHAPTER FOUR

1. Government of India, Ministry of Labour, *Agricultural Labour Inquiry* (New Delhi, 1952).

2. See, for example, Amiya Kumar Bagchi, "Foreign Capital and Economic Development in India: A Schematic View," in Kathleen Gough and Hari P. Sharma, eds., *Imperialism and Revolution in South Asia* (New York and London: Monthly Review Press, 1973), pp. 43-76.

3. Kamal Kumar Ghose, *Agricultural Labourers in India: A Study in the History of their Growth and Economic Condition* (Calcutta: Indian Publications, 1969). S. J. Patel, *Agricultural Labourers in Modern India and Pakistan* (Bombay: 1952).

4. Dharma Kumar, *Land and Caste in South India* (Cambridge: Cambridge University Press, 1965).

5. K. C. Alexander, *Social Mobility in Kerala* (Poona: Decan College Post-Graduate and Research Institute, 1968).

6. See K. R. Unni, "Sources of Agricultural Labour in Kerala: Some Social Perspectives," in Balakrishna N. Nair, ed., *Culture and Society* (Delhi: Thomson Press, 1975).

7. Ghose, *Agricultural Labourers in India;* Kathleen Gough, "Peasant Uprisings in India," manuscript, p. 45; R. P. Dutt, *India Today and Tomorrow* (Delhi: People's Publishing House, 1955), pp. 84-86.

8. T. C. Varghese, *Agrarian Change and Economic Consequences* (Bombay: Allied Publishers, 1970), p. 128.

9. The striking paradox here is that "land reforms" may have resulted in a decline in the raw number of those owning and

leasing land in a period of rapid increase of the population and especially of the population engaged in agriculture. It seems likely that some tenants have been evicted as a result of the land reforms or that some small cultivators have sold their land. (Kathleen Gough has pointed out to me that both these have occurred in Tanjore.) When we attempt to reconcile this with the previous observation in Chapter 1 that some small peasants and agricultural labourers in Kuttanad may be acquiring land, two conclusions seem to emerge: a) there has been increasing differentiation both among the cultivators and among the agricultural labourers; and b) there has been more downward than upward mobility.

10. As has been noted in Chapter 3, in 1971 Harijans made up 9.5 per cent of the total population of the district and 11 per cent of the population of the 52 Kuttanad villages. In 1961, 67 per cent of all Harijans and 83 per cent of the Pulayas (who are 60 per cent of the Harijans) were agricultural labourers. The Harijan proportion of agricultural labourers, however, is likely to be much higher than their proportion in the population because: a) the percentage of females among agricultural labourers is 40 as against 3 among cultivators and 22 among the non-agricultural work force; b) the census figures for Harijans do not include Harijans who have been converted to Christianity; and c) agricultural labourers generally enter the labour force at an earlier age.

11. It is estimated that there were 400,000 kudikidappukars in Kerala in 1970. As may be expected, their proportion was the highest in Alleppey district (27.7 per cent). See T. K. Oommen, "Agrarian Tension in a Kerala District." Of the 118 agricultural labourers in my survey, 82 were kudikidappukars.

12. There was nothing to prevent the landlord from taking away even his kudikidappukaran's personal crops if and when he so wished. And such instances were by no means uncommon. In this regard, one of the best loved poets of the Malayalam literature, Changampuzha (the "Shelley of Kerala") has a poignant story in his beautiful lyrical poem, *Vazhakula* (A bunch of bananas). The Pulaya of the poem plants a banana tree in his backyard. Day by day the family awaits the growth of the luscious fruits, only to have it snatched

away by the cruel landlord at the end. The poem ends with a powerful and foreboding warning which has had a lasting impact on the minds of generations of students in Kerala.

13. Pillai and Panikar, *Land Reclamation in Kerala* (New York: Asia Publishing House, 1965), p. 121.

14. These practices have been amply documented by such writers as J. H. Hutton, O'Malley, and Aiyappan. See my "Caste and Democracy in India," p. 38. "Ayyappan in 1937 gives a scale of distance pollution for several castes: a Nayar must keep 7 feet from a Namboothri Brahmin, an Iravan (Ilavan, Ishuvan, Tiyan) must keep 32, a Cheruman 64 and a Nayadi 74 to 124. The respective distances between these lower castes are calculated by a simple process of subtraction: the Iravan must keep 25 feet from the Nayar and Cheruman 32 feet from the Iravan," Srinivas, "The Caste System in India" in Andre Beteille, *Social Inequality* (Harmondsworth: Penguin, 1969), p. 268.

15. See below for more instances of such prejudice.

16. The "breast-cloth" controversy and riots are notorious in the history of Travancore. It ended in 1858 when the Raja gave formal permission to the lower caste women to wear upper garments. Tharamangalam, "Caste and Democracy in India," p. 38.

17. Some informants told me that occasional instances of some of these could be found until recently. It seems that even as late as ten or fifteen years ago an important Brahmin family in Kuttanad would not allow the Nair women who performed domestic tasks inside their house to wear upper garments.

18. Oommen, *Agrarian Tension*, p. 244. See also William H. Wiser's classical work on the Hindu Jajmani system, *The Hindu Jajmani System* (Lucknow, 1936).

19. A. V. Jose, "Wage Rates of Agricultural Labourers in Kerala," *Economic and Political Weekly*, Annual Number (February 1973).

20. Dandekar and Wrath, "Poverty in India," *Economic and Political Weekly* (Bombay), 2 January 1971, p. 38.

21. See especially P. K. Burdhan, "Green Revolution and Agricultural Labourers," *Economic and Political Weekly*, Special Number, July 1970; N. Krishnaji, "Wages of Agricultural Labour", *Eco-*

nomic and Political Weekly, 25 September 1971; and Robert W. Herdt and Edward A. Barker "Agricultural Wages, Production and the High-Yielding Varieties," *Economic and Political Weekly*, 25 March 1972.

22. A. V. Jose, "Trends in Real Wage Rates of Agricultural Labourers," *Economic and Political Weekly*, Review of Agriculture, 30 March 1974.

23. The increase in wage rates was 39 per cent in Alleppey district and 28 per cent in Palghat district. It remained less than 20 per cent in all other IADP districts. Burdhan's study has been used by some to argue that agrarian conflict in Kuttanad has no relationship to economic disparity or the Green Revolution. See, for instance, Oommen, *Agrarian Tension*.

24. Jose, "Wage Rates of Agricultural Labourers in Kerala."

25. P. G. K. Panikar, "Minute of Dissent," *Report of the Kuttanad Inquiry Commission* (Trivandrum, 1971), pp. 33-37.

26. A *kulian* is a local measure equal to 1/16th of a *para*, or .72 kg.

27. *Theerpu* was initially a payment meant only for migratory labourers who came from outside to participate in harvesting. These workers settled in the padashekharams until harvesting was over. In order to sustain themselves during these days they were given some sheaves of paddy immediately after harvesting, the actual amount varying from place to place.

28. Government of Travancore-Cochin, *Report of the Minimum Wages Committee for Employment in Agriculture* (Ernakulam, 1956), p. 8.

29. *Report of the Kuttanad Inquiry Commission Report*, p. 22.

NOTES TO CHAPTER FIVE

1. Interestingly, the leaders of the left already seem to have looked upon Kerala as a nation despite the political divisions and, as far as circumstances allowed, took the whole of Kerala as their unit in establishing and promoting their organizations.

2. The State Congress was the independent organization founded by the nationalists of Travancore when the Haripura session of the Indian National Congress banned all Congress activities in the princely states.

3. The government seems to have taken some measures to alleviate the situation. It made arrangements to provide rationed meals for 5 annas (about 1/3 of a rupee) in Alleppey and Shertallai and gave 5,000 tickets each to the unions in the two areas for distribution among the workers.

4. S. K. Das, "Kuttanattile Karshaka Thozhilali Sankhadana," *Thiruvitamkoor Kayar Factory Workers Union: Kanaka Jubilee Souvineer* [sic], (Quilon: Janayugam Press, 1972).

5. The Communist Party of India (Marxist) is locally referred to as the Marxist Party.

6. The local branch of the Anglican Church.

7. K. C. George, *Punnapra-Vayalar* (Trivandrum: Prabhat Book House, 1972).

8. All the facts relating to the planning and organization of the camps are difficult to establish and would require much more research than I have been able to conduct. The organizers and participants of the uprising claim that the camps developed spontaneously as the reign of terror unleashed by the police, the landlords, and their agents made life insecure for the labourers and their leaders. Although there is undoubtedly some truth in this, it also seems possible that the party's leadership saw the possibility of capturing power in the state through a Bolshevik-like uprising combined with a general strike throughout the state. The strike had clearly no immediate economic demands, which the leadership knew very well. For an account by a Communist partisan, see ibid.

9. The princely states of Travancore and Cochin both opted to join the Indian Union at the time of independence. They were combined together to form the state of Travancore-Cochin. The present state of Kerala came into existence in 1957 when the former Malabar district also joined Travancore-Cochin, thus bringing all the Malayalam-speaking people of the country into one state.

10. *Edangazhi* is a local measure equivalent to 1/10 of a para.

11. We have already referred to the liberation

struggle in Kerala. Para-military organizations of the kind mentioned here were organized all over the state, especially under the auspices of the Christian churches, even in places where there were no immediate threats from organized unions as in Kuttanad. In 1957-58 I was a personal witness to the organization of a unit of the "Christopher Volunteers" in a Catholic parish in a midland village in Kottayam district.

12. For a discussion of the split and its social and ideological background see Mohan Ram, *Indian Communism: Split Within a Split* (New Delhi: Vikas Publications, 1969).

13. The then president of the union is today a successful businessman who owns a holiday resort for the upper classes. He allegedly made his money when he was in charge of the "Labour Conduct Society" organized under the auspices of the government. It appears that he acted like a contractor in organizing work programmes to put up granite bunds along the sea coast, making enormous profits in the process.

14. This leader claimed that personal bitterness and vendetta were involved in this and that the police had been bribed to beat him up personally.

15. Oommen, *Agrarian Tension*, p. 257.

16. Ibid.

17. Nevertheless, the secretary of the KSKTU told me in 1974 that the union held 32 hectares of excess land in Alleppey district which was being cultivated by agricultural labourers. However, the location of this land could not be revealed. It is difficult to understand how so much land could be occupied and cultivated secretly.

18. *Report of the Kerala State Karshaka Thozhilabi Union (KSKTU) State Special Convention*, February 1975, p. 35.

19. A CPI(M) leader recently told me that the alliance with the Kerala Congress was a desperate attempt on the part of the party to win back the middle peasants who had been alienated from the party as a result of the violent struggles for kudikidappu land, which adversely affected their interests. This is a result of the basic ambiguity in the CPI(M)'s formulation of the tactical question of appropriate class alliances.

20. K. P. Joseph, "Strong and Extensive Excess Land Campaign in Alleppey District," *Karshaka Thozhilali*, May 1975, Alleppey, p. 23. Also from an interview with K. P. Joseph.

21. Local organizers complained that it was almost impossible to get even a few workers to participate in these struggles, especially on a working day. Before the campaign was launched, leaders had planned a tour of various centres in Kuttanad taluk where, at the receptions organized in their honour, they were to explain the nature and aims of the movement. I was present at two of those centres on two occasions. It was striking that those awaiting the leaders were no more than a handful and almost all of them were party or union officials. They had ready with them a *mala* (garland) for the leader of the tour party made of 100 one-rupee notes. In fact, they seemed to think they had accomplished their main task. I must hasten to add here that public meetings and rallies are a different matter. For these the CPI(M) can mobilize, even today, tens of thousands of people quite easily.

22. Kerala's CPI(M) leader, E. M. S. Namboothiripad, disagrees with the view that the campaign has been a failure. As early as 1972 he told the party's critics that the aim of the struggle was not to take over the excess land but to persuade the government to take it over and distribute it to the needy. The struggle was successful, he maintained, in so far as it unearthed the surplus land and obtained the moral support and participation of the masses. He reminds his critics that at the end of the salt satyagraha organized by Gandhi and the Congress there were people who wanted to measure its success in terms of the amount of salt collected, but urges them to remember that the British had to leave India as a result of such struggles. See *Chinta*, 13 October 1972.

NOTES TO CHAPTER SIX

1. See above p. 19. See also Kathleen Gough, "Imperialism and Revolutionary Potential," in Kathleen Gough and Hari, P. Sharma, eds., *Imperialism and Revolution in South Asia* (New York: Monthly Review Press, 1973), p. 12. For similar arguments about other areas in the country see Gough, "Peasant Resistance and Revolt in South India," *Pacific Affairs* (Winter 1968-69): 526-44. In a discussion of agrarian social structure in Tanjore, Beteille writes, "The extent of tenancy is on the decline and the tenants who remain will probably acquire greater economic security in the future. But the basic problem in the agrarian system continues to centre around the relationship between the landowners and the landless" ("Agrarian Relations in Tanjore District," *Studies in Agrarian Social Structure* [Oxford: Oxford University Press, 1974]).

2. Eric Wolf, *Peasant Wars of the Twentieth Century* (London: Faber and Faber, 1969), pp. 291 ff.; Hamza Alavi, "Peasants and Revolution," in Gough and Sharma, *Imperialism and Revolution in South Asia*, pp. 291-337.

3. See Kathleen Gough, "Peasant Resistance and Revolt in South India,"; Joan Mencher, "Agricultural Labour Unions: Some Socio-Economic and Political Considerations," paper presented at the IXth International Congress of Anthropological and Ethnological Sciences, Chicago, August-September 1973.

4. Eric Hobsbawm, "Class Consciousness in History," in I. Mészáros, *Aspects of History and Class Consciousness* (London: Routledge and Kegan Paul, 1971), p. 7.

5. Wolf, *Peasant Wars*.

6. For a discussion of the way in which "primordial loyalties mediate the process of peasant class mobilization," see Hamza Alavi, "Peasant Classes and Primordial Loyalties," *Journal of Peasant Studies* 1, no. 1 (1973): 23-61.

7. See, for instance, Joan Mencher, "The Caste System Upside Down, or the Not-So-Mysterious East," *Current Anthropology* 15, no. 4, (1974): 469.

8. In many places the Communists have been making use of already existing caste associations as bases of their own organizations. See Gough, "Peasant Resistance and Revolt in South India."

9. Eric Hobsbawm, "Peasants and Politics," *Journal of Peasant Studies* 1, no. 1 (1973): 11.

10. See, for example, Wolf, *Peasant Wars*, p. 294.

11. Especially worth comparing are the conditions of agricultural labourers in such states as Bihar and even Mysore in south India where even untouchability has not been eradicated. See, for instance, K. C. Alexander, *Seminar on Changing Agrarian Relations in India* (Hyderabad: National Institute of Community Development, 1974) and Arvind N. Das, "Agricultural Labour: In Bonded Freedom," *Economic and Political Weekly* (Bombay), 15 May 1976, p. 724.

12. In this respect, Lenin's distinction between trade union consciousness and socialist consciousness is well known. More recent attempts to distinguish various levels of class consciousness have been made by Antony Giddens, *The Class Structure of the Advanced Societies* (London: Hutchinson University Library, 1973), pp. 114 ff., and Michael Mann, *Consciousness and Action among the Western Working Class* (London: Macmillan, 1973).

13. "In the extreme case of what left-wing discussion has baptized 'substitutionism', the movement replaces the class, the party the movement, the apparatus of functionaries the party, the (formally elected) leadership the apparatus, and, in well known historical examples the inspired general secretary or the leader the central committee," Eric Hobsbawm, "Class Consciousness in History," in Mészaros, *Aspects of History and Class Consciousness*, p. 16.

14. Istvan Mészaros, "Contingent and Necessary Class Consciousness," in ibid., p. 98.

15. Communist Party of India (Marxist), "Resolution of the Central Committee: Tasks on the Trade Union Front," 1968, p. 2.

16. Ibid., p. 5.

17. Kathleen Gough, "Imperialism and Rev-

olutionary Potential in South Asia,'' in Gough and Sharma, *Imperialism and Revolution in South Asia*, p. 11.

18. Since the mid 1960's many militant cadres and supporters of the CPI(M) have left the party to form a number of Maoist formations in various parts of the country. For an account of these developments see Mohan Ram, *Maoism in India* (Delhi: Vikas Publications, 1971).

19. See Michael Mann, *Consciousness and Action among the Western Working Class*, for the view that integration itself takes various forms and that the degree of revolutionary consciousness and revolutionary potential is dependent on how integration takes place. While the social democrats have abandoned their goals of transforming society, radicals in France and Italy have been able to maintain a kind of class consciousness that still embodies a revolutionary consciousness.

Bibliography

Aiyappan, A. *Iraves and Culture Change*. Madras: Government Press, 1944.

Aiyer, Krishna S. Keralathile Sambadvyavastha. Trivandrum: Kerala Bhasta Institute, 1975.

Alavi, Hamza. "Peasant Classes and Primordial Loyalties." *Journal of Peasant Studies* 1, no. 1 (1973): 23-62.

______. "Peasants and Revolution." In *Imperialism and Revolution in South Asia*, edited by Kathleen Gough and Hari Sharma, pp. 291-337. New York and London: Monthly Review Press, 1973.

______. "India and the Colonial Mode of Production." *Economic and Political Weekly*, Special Number, August 1975.

Alexander, K. C. *Social Mobility in Kerala*. Poona: Deccan College Postgraduate Institute, 1968.

______. "Emerging Farmer-Labour Relations in Kuttanad." *Economic and Political Weekly*, 25 August 1973.

______. *Seminar on Changing Agrarian Relations in India*. Hyderabad: National Institute of Community Development, 1974.

______. "Land Reform Legislations in Kerala since Independence." *Behavioural Sciences and Community Development*, September 1974.

Alexandrov, Y. G. "Peasants, Development and Nationalism." In *Rural Protest, Peasant Movements and Social Change*, edited by H. Landsberger. London: Macmillan, 1973.

All India Kisan Sabha. "Agrarian Crisis in India and Tasks of Peasant Movement: Documents of the 22nd Conference." 1974.

Anonymous. "Agrarian Tension: How to Study it." Review of K. C. Alexander, *Agrarian Tension in Tanjavur*. *Economic and Political Weekly*, 18 September 1976.

Banaji, D. R. *Slavery in British India*. Bombay: Taraporevala, 1933.

Bendix, Reinhard, and S. M. Lipset. "Karl Marx's Theory of Social Classes." In *Class, Status and Power: Social Stratification in Comparative Perspective*, edited by Reinhard Bendix and S. M. Lipset. New York: Free Press, 1966.

Béteille, André. "Politics of Non-Antagonistic Strata." Delhi School of Economics, mimeographed, 1969.

__________. *Six Essays in Comparative Sociology*. Delhi: Oxford University Press, 1974.

__________. *Studies in Agrarian Social Structure*. Delhi: Oxford University Press, 1974.

Bottomore, T. B. *Karl Marx: Selected Writings in Sociology and Social Philosophy*. New York: McGraw Hill, 1964.

Buchanan, D. H. *Development of Capitalistic Enterprise in India*. New York: Macmillan, 1934.

Burdhan, P. K. "Green Revolution and Agricultural Labourers." *Economic and Political Weekly*, Special Number, July 1970.

Cockroft, J. D., A. G. Frank, and D. L. Johnson. *Dependence and Underdevelopment*. New York: Anchor Books, 1972.

Communist Party of India (Marxist): "Tasks on the Trade Union Front." Resolution of the Central Committee, 1968.

__________. *Central Committee Resolution on Certain Agrarian Issues and an Explanatory Note by P. Sundarayya*, n.d.

Cox, Oliver C. *Caste, Class and Race: A Study in Social Dynamics*. New York: Monthly Review Press, 1959.

Dahrendorf, Ralf. *Class and Class Conflict in Industrial Society*. Stanford: Stanford University Press, 1959.

Dalton, George. "Primitive, Archaic and Modern Economies: Karl Polany's Contribution to Economic Anthropology and Comparative Economy." In *Essays in Economic Anthropology*. Proceedings of the 1965 Annual Spring Meeting of the American Ethnological Society, edited by June Helum. Seattle: University of Washington Press, 1965.

Das, Arvind Narayan. "Agricultural Labour: In Bonded Freedom." *Economic and Political Weekly*, 15 May 1976.

Das, S. K. "Kuttanattile Karshaka Thozhilali Samkhadana." In *Thiruvitamkoor Kayar Factory Workers Union: Kanaka Jubilee Souvineer* [sic]. Quilon: Janayugam Press, 1972.

Desai, D. K. "Intensive Agricultural District Programme: Analysis of Results." *Economic and Political Weekly*, June 1969.

Dumont, Louis. "The Village Community: From Munro to Maine." *Contribution to Indian Sociology*, December 1966.

__________. *Homo Hierarchicus*. London: Weidenfeld and Nicholson, 1970.

Dutt, R. P. *India Today, and Tomorrow*. Delhi: Peoples' Publishing House, 1975.

Fischer, Ernst, and Franz Marek, eds. *The Essential Lenin*. New York: Herder and Herder, 1972.

Frankel, Francine. *India's Green Revolution: Economic Gains and Political Costs*. Bombay: Oxford University Press, 1971.

Geertz, Clifford. "Studies in Peasant Life: Community and Society." In *Biennial Review of Anthropology*, edited by B. J. Siegel. Stanford: Stanford University Press, 1962.

George, K. C. *Punnapra—Vayalar*. Trivandrum: Prabhat Book House, 1972.

Ghose, Kamal Kumar. *Agricultural Labourers in India: A Study in the History of their Growth and Economic Condition*. Calcutta: Indian Publications, 1969.

Giddens, Anthony. *The Class Structure of the Advanced Societies*. London: Hutchinson University Library, 1973.

Gopalan, A. K. *Kerala—Past and Present*. London: Lawrence and Wishart, 1959.

Gough, Kathleen. "Peasant Resistance and Revolt in South India." *Pacific Affairs* 41, no. 4 (Winter 1968-69): 526-44.

————. "Imperialism and Revolutionary Potential in South Asia." *Imperialism and Revolution in South Asia*, edited by K. Gough and H. P. Sharma, pp. 3-42. New York and London: Monthly Review Press, 1973.

————. "Peasant Uprisings in India." Manuscript, 1974.

————. "Indian Peasant Uprisings." *Bulletin of Concerned Asian Scholars* (July-September 1976).

Gough, Kathleen, and Hari P. Sharma, eds., *Imperialism and Revolution in South Asia*. New York and London: Monthly Review Press, 1973.

Gramsci, Antonio. *The Modern Prince and Other Writings*. London: Lawrence and Wishart, 1957.

Gunder Frank, Andre. *Capitalism and Underdevelopment in Latin America*. New York: Monthly Review Press 1967.

Hasbach, W. *A History of the English Agricultural Labourer*. London: Frank Case.

Herdt, Robert W., and Edward A. Baker. "Agricultural Wages, Production and the High-Yielding Varieties." *Economic and Political Weekly*, 25 March 1972.

Hobsbawm, Eric. "Peasants and Politics." *Journal of Peasant Studies* 1, no. 1 (1973): 3-21.

————. "Class Consciousness in History." In *Aspects of History and Class Consciousness*, edited by I. Mészaros. London: Routledge and Kegan Paul, 1971.

Howard, Louise E. *Labour in Agriculture: An International Survey*. London: Oxford University Press, 1935.

Hsiao-Tung, Fei. *Peasant Life in China*. London: Routledge and Kegan Paul, 1939.

Hsiao-Tung, Fei, and Chang-Chin I. *Earthbound China, A Study of Rural Economy in Yunnan*. London: Routledge and Kegan Paul, 1949.

Huizer, Gerrit. *The Revolutionary Potential of Peasants in Latin America*. Toronto: Lexington Books, 1972.

Hutton, J. H. *Caste in India*. 2nd ed. London: Oxford University Press, 1951.

India. Census Commissioner. *Census of India*. Travancore, 1931.

India. Census—1961, Kerala. *District Census Handbook, Alleppey*. Trivandrum, 1966.

India. Census—1971. Series 1, Paper 1, Supplement. *Provincial Population Totals*.

India. Census—1971. Series 9, Kerala. *District Census Handbook, Alleppey*. Trivandrum, 1973.

India. Labour Bureau. *Agricultural Labour in India*, 1969.

India. Ministry of Labour. *Report of the Agricultural Labour Inquiry Commission—Agricultural Wages in India*, vol. 1. Delhi: Manager of Publications, 1953.

Indian School of Social Sciences. "Agrarian Structure and Social Change in Selected Villages in Kerala: A Pilot Study of Three Villages." Manuscript. Trivandrum, 1973.

Indian Statistical Institute. *Macro-Regional Study of Kerala, 1959*. Mimeographed.

Jeffrey, Robin. *The Decline of Nayar Dominance: Society and Politics in Travancore, 1847-1908*. New York: Holmes and Meier, 1976.

Johl, S. S. "Gains of the Green Revolution: How They Have Been Shared in Punjab." *Journal of Development Studies*, April 1975.

Jose, A. V. "Wage Rates of Agricultural Labourers in Kerala." *Economic and Political Weekly* (Annual Number), February 1973.

______. "Trends in Real Wage Rates of Agricultural Labourers." *Economic and Political Weekly*, 30 March 1974.

Joseph, K. P. "Strong and Extensive Excess Land Campaign in Alleppey District." *Karshaka Thozhilali*, May 1975.

Karunakaran, Revi. *Message: Thiruvitamkoor Kayar Factory Workers Union: Kanaka Jubilee Survineer*. Janayugam Press, 1972.

Kerala, Bureau of Economics and Statistics. *Land Reform Survey in Kerala,* 1968.

————. ————. *Fact Book, on Agriculture.* Trivandrum, 1969.

————. ————. *The Third World Agricultural Census, 1970-71, Report for the Kerala State.*

————. *The Kerala Land Reforms Act, 1963.* Trivandrum, 1973.

————. *The Kerala Land Reforms (Ceiling) Rules, 1970* (as amended up to 5 May 1973) Trivandrum, 1973.

————. *The Kerala Land Reforms (Kudikidappukars Benefit Fund, Rules, 1970.* Trivandrum, 1973.

————. *The Kerala Land Reforms (Tenancy) Rules, 1970.* Trivandrum, 1970.

————. Punja Special Officer. "A Note on Kuttanad and Punja Cultivation."

————. *Report of the Kuttanad Inquiry Commission.* Trivandrum, 1971.

————. State Planning Board. *Economic Review Kerala, 1974.* Trivandrum, 1975.

————. ————. Evaluation Division, *Report on Intensive Agricultural District Programme in Kerala,* 1972.

Kerala State Karshaka Thozhilali Union. *Third Annual Report.* (Malayalam) 1973.

————. State Special Convention. *Report.* February 1975.

Koshy, Ninan. *Caste in the Kerala Churches.* The Christian Institute for the Study of Religion of Society. Bangalore, 1968.

Krishnaji, N. "Wages of Agricultural Labour." *Economic and Political Weekly,* 25 September 1971.

Kuhn, Thomas. *The Structure of Scientific Revolutions.* Chicago: University of Chicago Press, 1962.

Kumar, Dharma. *Land and Caste in South India.* Cambridge and London: Cambridge University Press, 1965.

Kuttanad Taluk Chettu Thozhilali Union. "Eleventh Annual Report", 1975. May 5 (Malayalam).

Laclau, Ernesto. "Feudalism and Capitalism in Latin America." *New Left Review* (May-June, 1971): 19-38.

Landsberger, Henry A., ed., *Rural Protest, Peasant Movements and Social Change*. London: Macmillan, 1973.

Leach, E. R. *Aspects of Caste in South India, Ceylon and North West Pakistan*. Cambridge: Cambridge University Press 1960.

Lefebvre, Henri. *The Sociology of Marx*. New York: Vintage, 1969.

Lenin, V. I. "A Great Beginning." In *Selected Works*, vol. 2. Moscow: Foreigr Language Publishing House, 1952.

_______. "The Agrarian Question and the 'Critics of Marx'." *Collected Works*, vol. 5. Moscow: Foreign Language Publishing House, 1961.

_______. *The Development of Capitalism in Russia* in *Collected Works*, vol. 3. Moscow: Foreign Language Publishing House, 1960.

_______. "To the Rural Poor." *Collected Works*., vol. 6. Moscow: Foreign Language Publishing House, 1961.

_______. "What is to be Done? Burning Questions of our Movement." In *Collected Works*, vol. 5. Moscow: Foreign Language Publishing House, 1961.

Lenski, Gerhard. *Power and Privilege: A Theory of Social Stratification*. New York: McGraw Hill, 1966.

Lewis, Oscar. *Life in a Mexican Village: Tepoztlan Restudied*. Urbana: University of Illinois Press, 1951.

Lipset, Seymour Martin. *Agrarian Socialism*. New York: Doubleday Anchor, 1950.

McEachern, Doug. "The Mode of Production in India." *Journal of Contemporary Asia* (1976): 444-57.

Mann, Michael. *Consciousness and Action among the Western Working Class*. London: Macmillan, 1973.

Marcuse, Herbert. *One Dimensional Man*. Boston: Beacon Press, 1964.

Marriott, McKim, ed., *Village India*. Chicago: University of Chicago Press, 1955.

Martinez-Alier, J. *Labourers and Landowners in Southern Spain*. London: Allen and Unwin, 1971.

Marx, Karl. "The Eighteenth Brumaire of Louis Bonaparte." *Selected Works* vol. 1, Moscow: Progress Publishers, 1969.

————. *Pre-Capitalist Economic Formations*. Edited by Eric Hobsbawm. New York: International Publishers, 1964.

Mencher, Joan. "Agricultural Labour Movements in their Socio-Political and Ecological Context: Tamil Nadu and Kerala" in Balakrishna N. Nair, ed., *Culture and Society*. Thomson Press, Delhi, 1975.

————. "Agricultural Labour Unions: Some Socio-Economic and Political Considerations." IXth International Congress of Anthropological and Ethnological Sciences. Chicago, August-September 1973.

————. "The Caste System Upside Down, or the Not-So-Mysterious East." *Current Anthropology*. December, 1974.

————. "Kerala and Madras: A Comparative Study of Ecology and Social Structure." *Ethnology* 5, no. 2 (1966): 135-71.

————. "Limitations of Flexibility and their Implications for the Creation of a Socialist State: The Case of Kerala." Paper presented at the Annual Meeting of the American Anthropological Association, Toronto, 1972.

Menon, K. P. Padmanabha. *History of Kerala*, 3 vols., Madras, 1924.

Mészaros, Istvan, ed., *Aspects of History and Class Consciousness*. London: Routledge and Kegan Paul, 1971.

————. "Contingent and Necessary Class Consciousness." In *Aspects of History and Class Consciousness,* edited by I. Mészaros. London: Routledge and Kegan Paul, 1971.

Mintz, Sidney. "Canamelar: The Sub-culture of a Rural Sugar Plantation Proletariat." In *The People of Puerto Rico*, edited by J.H. Stewart et al. Urbana: University of Illinois Press, 1956.

________. "The Folk-Urban Continuum and the Rural Proletarian Community" *American Journal of Sociology* 59, no. 2 (1953): 136-43.

________. "The Rural Proletariat and the Problem of Rural Proletarian Consciousness." *Journal of Peasant Studies* 1, no. 1 (1973): 91-106.

Moore, Barrington, Jr., *Social Origins of Dictatorship and Democracy: Lord and Peasant in the Making of the Modern World*. Boston: Beacon Press, 1966.

Mouzelis, N. "Capitalism and the Development of Agriculture." *Journal of Peasant Studies* 3, no. 4 (1976): 483-92.

Myrdal, Gunnar. *Asian Drama: An Inquiry into the Poverty of Nations*. New York: Pantheon, 1968.

Nair, Balakrishna N., ed., *Culture and Society*. Delhi: Thomson Press, 1975.

Namboothiripad, E. M. S. *Athma Katha*. Trivandrum. Deshaphimani Book House, 1970.

________. *The National Question in Kerala*. Delhi: People's Publishing House, 1952.

________. *The Peasant in National Economic Construction*. Delhi: People's Publishing House, 1954.

________. "Replies to Questions," *Chinta*, 13 October 1972.

National Council of Applied Economic Research, *The Techno-Economic Survey of Kerala*. New Delhi, 1962.

Nicholas, Ralph. "Structure and Politics in Villages of Southern Asia." In *Structure and Change in Indian Society*, edited by Milton Singer and Bernard Cohn. Chicago: Aldine Atherton, 1968.

Omvedt, Gail. "Development of the Maharashtrian Class Structure, 1818-1931." *Economic and Political Weekly*, Special Number, 1973.

Oommen, T. K. "Agrarian Tension in a Kerala District: An Analysis." Sri Ram Center for Industrial Relations. Reprint Series, no. 15. [New Delhi].

________. "FAO Survey on Peasant Organization in India: The Case of Alleppey." Center for the Study of Social Systems, Jawaharlal Nehru University. New Delhi, 1974.

————. "Green Revolution and Agrarian Conflict." *Economic and Political Weekly*, 26 June 1971.

Ossowski, Stanislaw. *Class Structure in the Social Consciousness*. New York: The Free Press of Glencoe, 1963.

Panikar, P. G. K. "Minute of Dissent." *Report of the Kuttanad Inquiry Commission*. Trivandrum, 1971.

Panikkar, K. M. *A History of Kerala 1498-1801*. Annamalainagar: Annamalai University Press, 1960.

Patel, Surrendra J. *Agricultural Labourers in Modern India and Pakistan*. Bombay, 1952.

Pillai, V. R. and P. G. K. Panikar. *Land Reclamation in Kerala*. New York: Asia Publishing House, 1965.

Pillai, T. K. Velu. *State Manual of Travancore*, 4 vols. Trivandrum, 1940.

Post, Kent. " 'Peasantization' and Rural Political Movements in Western Africa." *European Journal of Sociology* 13, no. 2 (1972): 223-54.

Pothan, S. G. *The Syrian Christians of Kerala*. Bombay: Asia Publishing House, 1963.

Ram, Mohan. *Indian Communism: Split Within a Split*. New Delhi: Vikas Publications, 1969.

————. *Maoism in India*. New Delhi: Vikas Publications, 1971.

Rao, V. K. R. V., ed., *Agricultural Labour in India: Seminar on 2nd Agricultural Labour Inquiry*. New York: Asia Publishing House, 1962.

Redfield, Robert. *Tepoztlan, a Mexican Village: A Study of Folk Life*. Chicago: University of Chicago Press, 1930.

Rhodes, I. Robert. *Imperialism and Underdevelopment*. New York and London: Monthly Review Press, 1970.

Rudolph, Lloyd I., and Susanne H. Rudolph. *The Modernity of Tradition* Chicago: University of Chicago Press, 1967.

Rudra, Ashok, M. M. Mukopadhyaya. "Hiring of Labour by Poor Peasants." *Economic and Political Weekly*, 10 January 1976.

Saith, Ashwani, and Ajay Tankha. "Agrarian Transition and the Differentiation of the Peasantry: A Study of a West U. P. Village." *Economic and Political Weekly*, 1 April 1972.

Sastri, K. A. Nilakanta. *A History of South India*. Madras: Oxford University Press, 1955.

Scott, C. D. "Peasants, Proletarianization and the Articulation of Modes of Production: The Case of Sugar-Cane Cutters in Northern Peru, 1940-1969." *Journal of Peasant Studies* 3, no. 3 (1976): 321-42.

Shanin, Teodor. *The Awkward Class: Political Sociology of Peasantry in a Developing Society, Russia 1910-1925*. London: Oxford University Press, 1972.

________. "Peasantry: Delineation of a Sociological Concept and a Field of Study." *European Journal of Sociology* 12 (1971).

________. *Peasants and Peasant Societies*. Harmondsworth: Penguin, 1971.

Sharma, Hari P. "The Green Revolution in India, Prelude to a Red One?" In *Imperialism and Revolution in South Asia*, edited by K. Gough and H. P. Sharma, pp. 77-102. Monthly Review Press, 1973.

Shea, Thomas W. J. "Agrarian Politics of Land Reform in Malabar." Manuscript. 1956.

Silverberg, James, ed., *Social Mobility in the Caste System in India, an Interdisciplinary Symposium*. The Hague: Mouton, 1968.

Srinivas, M. N. "The Caste System in India." In André Béteille, ed. *Social Inequality*. Harmondsworth: Penguin, 1969.

Srinivas, M. N., and A. M. Shah. "The Myth of the Self-Sufficiency of the Indian Village." *Economic and Political Weekly* (Special Number), 1960.

Stavenhagen, Rodolfo. *Agrarian Problems and Peasant Movements in Latin America*. New York: Doubleday, 1970.

————. *Social Classes in Agrarian Societies*. New York: Doubleday Anchor, 1975.

Stinchcombe, Arthur L. "Agricultural Enterprise and Rural Class Relations." *American Journal of Sociology* 67, no. 2 (1961): 165-76.

Tampi, A. N. *Economic Survey of Travancore*, 1941.

Tharamangalam, J. "Caste and Democracy in India." M. A. thesis, Department of Sociology, York Unviersity, 1972.

Thorner, Daniel. *The Agrarian Prospect in India*. Delhi: Delhi University Press, 1956.

Thorner, Daniel, and Alice Thorner. *Land and Labour in India*. Bombay: Asia Publishing House, 1965.

Thurston, E. *Castes and Tribes of Southern India*, 7 vols. Madras Government Press, 1909.

Travancore Census Commissioner. *Census of Travancore, 1891*.

Travancore-Cochin. *Report of the Minimum Wages Committee for Employment in Agriculture, 1956*. Ernakulam, 1965.

Tse-tung, Mao. "How to Analyse the Classes in Rural Areas." In *Selected Works*. New York: International Publishers, 1954.

Unni, K. Raman. "Sources of Agricultural Labour in Kerala. Some Social Perspectives." In *Culture and Society*, edited by Balakrishna N. Nair. Delhi: Thomson Press, 1975.

Varghese, T. C. *Agrarian Change and Economic Consequences*. Bombay: Allied Publishers, 1970.

Wiser, William H. *The Hindu Jajmani System*. Lucknow, 1936.

Wolf, Eric. "On Peasant Rebellions" in Theodor Shanin, *Peasants and Peasant Societies*. Harmondsworth: Penguin, 1971.

————. *Peasant Wars of the Twentieth Century*. London: Faber and Faber, 1969.

Zagoria, Donald S. "The Ecology of Peasant Communism in India." *American Political Science Review* 65, no. 1 (1971): 144-60.

Zeitlin, Maurice. *Revolutionary Politics and the Cuban Working Class*. Princeton: Princeton University Press, 1967.

Index